Praise for *Standing O! Encore*

"*Standing O!* and now *Standing O! Encore* reinforce something we all need more of- gratitude. Each day I'm thankful for two entire books dedicated to giving thanks."
- *Marc Hodulich, Entrepreneur, featured in* **Sports Illustrated,** *The Wall Street Journal &* **ESPN,** *endurance athlete*

"Inspirational, motivational, heart-warming and thought provoking. The stories inside *Standing O!* and *Standing O! Encore* are uplifting and packed full of grace. What makes these books so special are all of the servant led minds behind each and every story. Givers give and this is what makes these books so special. *Standing O!* & *Standing O! Encore* are must reads for daily motivation."
- *Larry Levine, co-founder Social Sales Academy, bestselling author of* **Selling from the Heart** *and* **Standing O!** *contributor*

"Back & better than before, they've done it again. *Standing O! Encore* has compiled some more amazing life journeys that are definitely worth the read."
- *Marq Brown, former Auburn Tiger, New York Jet, personal trainer & endurance athlete*

"*Standing O! Encore* is another tremendous way for people with Dreams and Goals to be encouraged. The stories are inspiring and uplifting. People will thank you when you get them a copy."
- *Robert Owens, international keynote speaker, adventurer, business consultant, ironman, special ops pararescueman*

"The stories in *Standing O! Encore* once again pack a motivational punch that can lift your spirits everyday. That is why I have given copies of the original *Standing O!* to family and friends as gifts and recommended it to my clients as well!"
- *Dave Anderson, CEO, speaker, trainer, author of* **Becoming a Leader of Character - Six Habits that Make or Break a Leader at Work and at Home**

"Amazing book! Gratitude is the answer and *Standing O! Encore* wrote the book on it! A must read!"
- *Heather Monahan, CEO, best-selling author and podcast host of 5*

"I never thought that getting lost in Manhattan would lead me to writing a chapter in a book - and to be able to share with the world the strength of resilience of my dear friend KP, a doctor who fights HIV and AIDS in rural Botswana - all while contributing to a good cause supporting youth here in NYC! It's exciting to see even more inspiring stories in *Standing O! Encore.*"
                    - Talia Mota, leading scientist on a mission to cure HIV

"*Standing O! Encore* is about inspiration. Taking people's inspirational stories and passing them on to inspire the next generation."
    - Tim Hughes, CEO of Digital Leadership Associates #1 social selling pioneer
                                        & innovator, keynote speaker

"This is a powerful read that salutes the special people who have taught us so many of life's important lessons. It will leave you with a mountain of positive energy!"
        - Marc Megna, former New England Patriot, owner of Anatomy

"Truly compelling collection. Read *Standing O! Encore* to be motivated!"
    - Mark Moyer, CEO, business & career coach for athletes and entreprenuers,
                                author & host of **Make Your Mark**

"*Standing O! Encore* is an incredible testament to the concept that life is a team sport. EVERYONE benefits by leaning on and learning from others to get where they want to go - in both helping address challenges, and in exploring opportunities. Each essay from the accomplished contributors reinforces these themes, with proceeds supporting incredible causes."
        - Bradley T. Mason, vice president, Fiserv, chairman of the board New Image
                            Youth Center & founder of The Give Team

"Every chapter in *Standing O! Encore* reveals the three keys to psychological strength: Inward. Outward. Forward."
        - Stacy Feiner, PsyD, CEO of Psynamics, business psychologist, Forbes
                            contributor, author of **Talent Mindset**

"It only takes one person to believe in you and this book exemplifies the gratitude that is felt towards these fantastic individuals!"
    - Jen Fitzpatrick, founder FEMM International, co-founder Hero Intelligence
                                    Agency, author, TEDx speaker

"Participating in the creation of *Standing O!* helped me communicate to my parents my gratitude of the sacrifices they made for my sister and me. Presenting the book to my Mom for her 83rd birthday brought tears of appreciation and joy no materialistic birthday gift could ever match. Deepest Thanks to Scott Macgregor for the privilege to contribute to such a great cause."
                            - Mike Sadeghpour, founder of edgeThink

"If you enjoyed the fifty plus stories of gratitude and life changing lessons in *Standing O!*, you are going to be blown away by what you find in *Standing O! Encore*. Standing O! Nation continues to inspire and educate while contributing in a real, tangible way to the development of young people in some of our nation's most underprivileged neighborhoods. Great book. Great causes."

— *Matt McDarby, author of* **Cadence of Excellence**

"So excited about this body of work. In a time when there is so much negativity, *Standing O! Encore* delivers a powerful punch of positivity and gratitude x 53! Great work Scott MacGregor for another awesome collaboration."

— *Steve Nudelberg, CEO of* **On the Ball**, *speaker, trainer, author*

grat-i-tude:
the quality of being thankful, readiness to show appreciation for and
return kindness

"No one who achieves success does so without the help of others. The
wise and confident acknowledge this help with gratitude."
– Alfred North Whitehead

Standing O! Encore

A collection of essays from successful people
about the role models who inspired them

Eaton Press

EatonPress.com

Table of Contents

Dedicated to:

The incredible team at SomethingNew who dedicate their time and talent to make our company successful and in turn allow us to make the world a better place. Your hard work, integrity and dedication is something I treasure. Thank you for believing in me and more importantly in our mission to #DoSomethingGood. You guys rock!!

Preface - Scott MacGregor

Scott MacGregor is the founder & CEO of SomethingNew LLC, one of the fastest-growing talent strategy companies in the country. SomethingNew is a four-time recipient of the American Business Award for Innovation. Beyond finding clients exceptional talent, SomethingNew's advisory services called SomethingNew Labs™ saves companies millions of dollars through teaching and providing proprietary tools centered on three pillars of an effective people strategy: talent acquisition, onboarding and retention. MacGregor's belief that good companies do good things led him to establish SomethingGood™, which is the social mission component of SomethingNew. His first book, Standing O! *and now* Standing O! Encore *are part of that mission as all of the proceeds go to charity.*

. . . .

The power of gratitude for me comes from scarcity and tough times, not from abundance and the easy road.

- I am grateful to have grown up without the wealth that was surrounding me.

- I am grateful for the work I had to do to keep our house heated by chopping, splitting, and stacking wood nonstop.

- I am grateful for working in my dad's gas station from when I was ten years old.

- I am grateful for coaches who pushed me to the brink.

- I am grateful for teachers who demanded more.

- I am grateful for relationships that didn't work out.

- I am grateful for physical setbacks.

At the time, I may have hated all these things, but viewing them now from the rearview mirror, I realize that I owe all my happiness and success to them. Diamonds are created from pressure and pearls from the constant irritant of a grain of sand or a parasite (bet you didn't know that). The mountains my wife and I enjoy climbing were formed from massive disruption. The beaches we love to walk on came from the unrelenting pounding of the sea. As I get older, I get less frustrated by tough times because I know now that you see the rainbow after the storm, not before the storm. You see the gains after the suffering.

Gratitude is a state of mind. As Lou Gehrig famously said in the face of a terminal disease: "Today I consider myself the luckiest man on the face of the Earth." I am incredibly grateful to so many people who have impacted my life and made every triumph possible. Please enjoy our fifty-three inspirational contributing authors as they give a "Standing O!" to those who shaped their lives.

Foreword - Heather Monahan

Heather Monahan is a bestselling author, keynote speaker, entrepreneur, and founder of Boss in Heels. She is one of the few women to break the glass ceiling and claim her spot in the C-suite. She currently works with Fortune 500 companies and professional athletes to develop confidence in the workplace and on the court. Her work has been featured in USA Today, CNN, Forbes, Fast Company, *and* Business News Daily. *Her new book,* Confidence Creator, *shot to number one on Amazon's business biographies and business motivation lists, and her podcast,* Creating Confidence, *debuted in the top 200 shows on Apple Podcasts.*

. . . .

I can't believe I am sitting here writing the foreword for *Standing O! Encore.* I need to take you back three years with me for you to fully understand the role gratitude has played in my life.

Three years ago, I was a C-suite executive in corporate America, responsible for hundreds of millions of dollars and hundreds of employees across the country. Over the fourteen years I had worked for that company, I had been promoted three times and had won many awards. In July 2017, I was named one of the most influential women in radio. On July 27, 2017, I was fired in a meeting that took less than five minutes. To say I was in shock is an understatement. The CEO I had worked for had become ill and stepped down, and his daughter had been elevated to replace him. It didn't take her any time to call me in and let me know that I was no longer needed and my position was eliminated.

The three-hour drive home after that meeting was horrible. As a single mother, I felt panicked and distraught. In that moment, I felt I had lost everything. I had no idea where I would go, what I would do, or how I would replace my income. Things seemed incredibly bleak. One of the first things I did was to post on social media and let my network know I had been fired and I was really hurting. A number of people told me this was a bad idea; however, I decided to listen to my instinct and keep the post up. This was a fantastic idea, and I was grateful that I listened to my intuition.

Immediately, I received countless offers of help, ideas, and support. I decided to see being fired as putting me in good company. The stories flooded in as others shared how being fired had changed their lives for the better. I began to have hope. It was then that I decided to lean on my gratitude practice as part of my daily routine. Not only would I write down three things that I was grateful for, but I would also record all the small wins that would occur in the weeks after I was fired. I started to see that just because I didn't know what was going to happen next didn't mean it wouldn't be amazing.

Day after day, I would see positive people showing up for me, and I was shocked. I realized that when I fired the villain in my life, I created space for amazing people to show up and support me. Clearing negativity and toxic people from your life allows for space that welcomes grateful and positive people to come in. During that time, I began writing. Initially, I wrote about the evil villain and how I loathed her, but over time it morphed into chapters of my life's lowest moments and how I learned to create confidence from each one of them. Suddenly, I was going to be an author for the first time in my life.

To say this was scary for me is an understatement. I had no idea how my book would be received, if I would be sued, or if anyone would ever buy a copy. I found an editor and began the self-publishing process. These days were tough because I constantly struggled with the idea of not really being an author. After a lifetime in sales and sales leadership, I didn't know if I could be anything else. The day finally came to publish my book, and so many people tried to put their self-limiting beliefs on me to protect me, but I forged forward and released Confidence Creator into the world while I hid under a weighted blanket waiting for the worst to happen.

After hiding for a day under a blanket, I decided to rise up and do what I had always done: hustle, promote, and sell my product and myself. That means pitching every bookstore to take your book in, speaking anywhere and everywhere you can to spread the message of your book, and going on countless podcasts and shows to attempt to cut through the clutter and make others aware of your book. This part of the process was the grind, and it certainly consumed every minute of my day.

During this time, I was in need of a contact at New York University, so I went to my Linkedin contacts and typed in "NYU." Scott MacGregor's name popped up, and I sent him a message. He was so gracious to connect me to his contacts at NYU. He and I became fast friends, and when I shared with him about my new book and initiative to take it to the top, he asked if I would like to be a contributing author in a book he was working on titled Standing O. At this time, I was an author technically, but I certainly didn't feel like one yet. I still felt like a fraud in some regards. Scott assured me that his book was for charity and bringing good into the world and all I needed to do was to write one chapter about someone I was grateful for.

I thought about it for one minute and felt so grateful for Scott helping me when he didn't know me that it became an easy answer. Yes, I would write a chapter, even though I didn't know if it would be any good and I was time-strapped. I would go for it because I was grateful for his support and help.

Surprisingly, writing that one chapter made it even more official that I was an author, and it helped me get over that fraud mindset I was stuck in. I began seeing that being grateful drives you to make decisions that put you in amazing places. Yes, I was now an author and about to be a contributing author, and that made me feel proud. Yes, I would want to support Scott's book launch and help in any way I could. Yes, spending time helping those who support you and treat you well creates magic in life, and for that I felt very grateful.

Scott had explained there was a book launch happening in New York City and he really wanted my support in attending. At that same time, I received a message from an NBA player who had read my book. He said the book had really opened his eyes, and he needed to meet with me before the basketball season started. Yet again, I felt intimidated and wondered if I could help a professional athlete. Yet again, my fraud mindset crept back in. I attempted to use Scott's book launch party as an excuse for why I couldn't make a face-to-face meeting. The player's agent was so happy because by chance they were scheduled to be in New York the same day. Yet again, showing up to help others puts you in absolutely the right place for you to be.

Beyond nervous and intimidated, I forced myself out of my hotel room and headed to the lobby to meet up with the player and his agent. Walking into the lounge and seeing this young man clutching my book to his chest made me think of my son, and suddenly I knew I would help him in some way. The agent left us alone to talk. The player began to explain to me how in practice he was unstoppable, but somehow when he took the court during a game, he was a fraction of the player he knew he had the potential to be. He then explained to me that one thing that really differentiated the best in the league and the rest was confidence, and he needed some.

We talked about many things that afternoon, including firing the villains from his life and putting himself first. We talked about writing reminders on his shoes so he never forgets what he really is capable of at any time. Then we talked about gratitude. Instead of feeling like the whole world is watching you, what if instead you focus on one child and feel grateful to have the chance to inspire him to reach his goals and become his best? What if you lowered that pressure on yourself and remembered that you really love this game and you can be grateful for the opportunity to go out there and do what you love every day? What if we took our focus off the outcome and put it on gratitude instead?

Our meeting was going great. I looked at my watch and saw that I was late for Scott's book launch. I immediately excused myself from the meeting, hopped in a cab, and headed to Philippe Guggenheim's HG Contemporary gallery. Arriving at the launch was so exciting. Scott and his whole team welcomed me with open arms and were so grateful that I had made it. I met so many like-minded people who were all interested in helping others and supporting one another. Seeing gratitude in motion is a really special feeling.

Since that night, so many things have happened as a result of gratitude and my newfound friendship with Scott. I no longer feel like a fraud. I wake up every day living a life with purpose and passion and surrounding myself with others who do the same. No, every day is not easy, but on those days when things aren't easy, I have an amazing crew I can reach out to knowing they will pick me up when I am down. I wake up excited for each day, never knowing what amazing opportunity or experience may appear.

Over that next year, Scott would introduce me to countless people who would help me in my business. He would advocate for me to be a speaker at massive events where he knew someone in charge. Sometimes things would work and sometimes they wouldn't, but that didn't matter. Realizing that I have a friend who has my back at every turn would take me back to my gratitude, and as soon as that would happen, something spectacular would show up. Being open to helping others and meeting new people has brought so much into my life, and I never anticipated any of it.

One day a few months ago, I woke up to a text message asking if I would be willing to write the foreword for the new book *Standing O! Encore*. I had tears in my eyes. It would be such an honor. I immediately was overwhelmed with gratitude. Today, I no longer feel like a fraud. Gratitude, great friends, and giving back have changed my life, and I am hopeful this book will change yours for the better.

Introduction - Jaime Lannon Diglio

Jaime Lannon Diglio is president of SomethingNew LLC, one of the fastest-growing talent strategy firms in the country and four-time recipient of the American Business Award for Innovation. Before joining the SomethingNew team, she held sales leadership roles at Microsoft and Gartner. She shifted her career to shine a spotlight on how to win the war for talent by intentionally investing in people as the key to long-term growth. Through SomethingNew Labs, Diglio advises CEOs on how to rewire, hire, and inspire their teams.

. . . .

I'm grateful for my struggle because, from it, I have found my strength.

When Scott MacGregor asked me to write this introduction, I was incredibly honored and, at the same time, felt pressure to write something that encompassed the gratitude I feel to be part of the Standing O! mission. I'm the first to raise my hand and say, "I'm not a writer, which is why I listen and talk for a living."

I've never written an introduction to a book before, so I did what I always do when I feel stuck: I consulted my nine-year-old daughter, Kaylin. "I'm writing the introduction to our book, which is all about gratitude for life lessons and learning from people and experiences and how they make us stronger," I told her.

She replied, "Wait, you're writing it, and it's a book you can buy? Cool!" I smiled and said, "You learned about gratitude in school. What do you think it means? How would you explain it?"

She quickly did a backflip, fixed her ponytail, and said: "Gratitude is a gift, but you have to focus on it to see it."

Seeing tomorrow's sun through today's clouds is the hardest part, but it's a habit worth forming.

Real is never perfect, and perfect is never real.

Today we live in a world that promotes perfection. We've entered the "me" era with fantasies of achieving the perfect body, perfect kids, and perfect friends while choosing the perfect career path, building the perfect business with the perfect people, and having enough money and time to perfectly do it all, showing it off in a perfect social media post.

We are obsessed with being the next "overnight" sensation. The mirror we use to measure ourselves and others is bigger than ever. We want results fast, and when things don't go as planned, it's easy to give up. The rate of people dropping out of relationships, jobs, sports, and schools is at an all-time high, and this isn't a coincidence.

We've come to a tipping point, and it's too much to keep up with everything. People are burned out at work and in life, pretending to put on a strong front yet suffering in silence. In this "me" era, we want it all immediately and have lost sight of the reality that perfect isn't real and great things take time.

The good news is that those who will survive and thrive in this new world are the people who focus on what they already have, not what they don't. The more you are grateful, the more you attract things to be thankful for.

I am grateful for work I've done to see beyond the surface in myself and others.

Nothing worth doing is ever easy.

Very few people are talking about the journey—the bumps and bruises, the failures, the starts and stops. The behind-the-scenes look at how success is really created. The winners in this new era understand that success is not about measuring your progress using someone else's ruler. It's created by people who intentionally keep going when things get really hard. These people choose courage over comfort and are willing to sit in discomfort because they believe in what they are doing. They remind themselves why they started and keep pushing forward. They dig in and build grit. They show up as their authentic selves and focus less on knowing it all and more on learning it all.

I am grateful to those who encouraged me to keep going.

Make lemons out of lemonade.

The strongest people I have met have not come from an easy past. When I connect the dots in my life, I see that every challenge is now a gift I carry forward with me. This collection of gifts has made me stronger. I believe that life is a series of lessons, and with each one, we come closer to who we are meant to be. In the spirit of this book, I would like to share some of my lessons with you. I choose to look at them not as failures but as stepping stones to lead me forward. My mom always said, "When you've got lemons, make lemonade."

I am grateful to have had a mom who pushed me to play bigger, even when I wanted to hide.

What makes some people rise and others fall?

I've always been obsessed with understanding what motivates people and how they think, especially when life gets hard and things don't go as expected. What keeps them moving forward? My curiosity about understanding people started when I was an awkward, overweight kid who felt misunderstood. I struggled in school and learned to compensate by talking with the teachers and doing whatever I could to earn extra credit. I realized early on that I wasn't going to achieve my goals the traditional way, so I had to put in the work and create "nontraditional" ways to succeed. I found sports, and on the soccer field, I learned how to work hard, communicate, and motivate people forward. The more I talk with people, the more I realize that my story is not uncommon. How do you push past the labels given to you and design your unique path for success?

I'm grateful that when people said I wasn't good enough, I dared to say, "Watch me."

All we have to do is take the first step.

My curiosity about how people choose to step forward or stay stuck during times of tragedy peaked as a young woman working in New York City on 9/11. I sat anchored in my own fear and surrounded by a sea of sadness. I had only been living and working in the city for about a year when tragedy struck, and I lost my job. It was a time when I, like people all over the world, felt fear and emotions never experienced before. I remember having so much gratitude for being alive and selfishly having an enormous concern about not having a job. My parents begged me to move back home to Boston, but I chose to stay. I had an inner voice encouraging me to step forward and keep going.

I'm grateful that I didn't choose the easy way out and was determined to figure it out.

Everything happens for a reason.

I didn't have a job and needed to pay my bills, so I decided to waitress and bartend at a local sports bar. Going from wearing a suit to waiting tables was not how I envisioned my career path. Now that I look back, it was a humbling experience that made me stronger because it forced me out of my comfort zone. I learned how to talk to all types of customers and connect with them. It taught me empathy and the fundamentals of selling. I became so fascinated with people and their motivations that I decided to earn my master's degree in organizational psychology. I knew that understanding how people move within organizations, teams, and systems was the key to driving change. Business is about knowing how to connect with people.

I'm grateful that I checked my ego at the door and got to work.

When we look back, we discover life was never random. It is all connected.

I eventually joined the world's leading research and advisory firm and moved from marketing to sales, where I built a multimillion-dollar business from scratch in a new market. I attribute my success to my ability to understand people, and it compounded through word of mouth. When you do an excellent job for customers, they naturally tell others. No tricks. No fancy advertising and scripts. You deliver what you promise. Everything I learned while waitressing and bartending I used in business.

I'm grateful I could prove that customers are just people who are looking for someone to trust and listen.

Our differences make us stronger.

Business kept growing, so I had to hire. My recruiting strategy, like my past, was a bit unorthodox but hugely successful. I looked for the people who pivoted in their careers, chose hard paths, and talked about their struggles. I sought out baseball players, not people who just looked good in the uniform. I wanted the people with scars, who color outside the lines, and who have the courage to be themselves in a perfectly imperfect way. I created teams that were diverse in their strengths and backgrounds. I hired former teachers, consultants, recruiters, athletes, and military service members to complement those with traditional sales backgrounds. I was consistently building the top teams that everyone wanted to be on. Success did not come from any individual's strength but instead resulted from how team members' unique abilities complemented one another and how they were integrated into a team that could attack. We are always better together.

I'm grateful I understood that having different views builds long-term strength.

When you see something, say something.

I spent the last fifteen years leading teams in two of the most well-known companies on the planet and helping hundreds of organizations keep up with the rapidly changing technology landscape. I advised leaders on how to embrace uncertainty and digitally transform their businesses. I learned how to get comfortable with being uncomfortable as the only woman in the room. I also noticed something that was happening over and over again, regardless of the company size or industry. A group of leaders would focus on promises of new processes and technology, but nobody was talking about the people.

I would repeatedly be the one person at the table saying, "All this planning and tech investment is great. What's your strategy to bring your people on board and support all this change?"

Nine times out of ten, my question was ignored until the leader would come back to me and say, "Hey, my people are not cooperating; I could use your help."

I'm grateful that I spoke up and had the courage to talk about what others avoided.

You can't see the picture when you're in the frame.

We've forgotten that companies are collections of people. We've overlooked how to take care of ourselves and each other at work and at home. The over-emphasis on technology as a promise to improve everything has made leaders undervalue people and overvalue process and technology. I've been studying people, motivation, and change for the last fifteen years, and the pendulum is finally starting to swing back. Talented people are among the hardest resources to find and keep. It's as if we've lost touch with the basics of being a human being at work. People want support at work and need to feel valued, seen, and heard. Leadership is not about telling people what to do; it's helping people think about their thinking.

We are not hiring robots; we're hiring people with lives outside work. How we show up at work is a reflection of how we show up at home, and how we show up at home is a reflection of how we show up at work. If we want to have the best team, we need to support those people across their entire lives. Nobody helps me see this more than my husband when he is coaching his high school cross-country team. Year over year, the kids perform at their peak because he focuses on the whole kid, not just the kid in the race.

I'm grateful for all of the people who have challenged me about what stays at work and what stays at home.

We can't go back, but we can start where we are and design our future.

You might wonder why I'm so passionate about supporting people in the workplace. It's because I, too, had my tipping point. As a working mom, I had created what I call a "culture bubble" around my teams and was trying to hold it all together. I was supporting everyone at work but felt like no one supported me. I was trying to pour from an empty cup. My mom told me many times: "Jaime, you're going to burn out," and like most people, I didn't change until I was forced to.

My tipping point happened in 2015 when my kids were four and two years old. I was in the middle of a client meeting, and my legs went completely numb. After spending two days at Yale New Haven Hospital and being evaluated by four doctors, they couldn't figure out what was wrong with me. When you're a young, healthy person, you start to wonder, "Is this in my head?" It's hard to explain unless you've been through something similar. I'm sharing this part of my story because despite being a frightening time, it woke me up and led me to where I am today. I am thankful because it showed me that I needed to pay attention and re-evaluate who I was, what I was doing, and where I stood (literally and figuratively).

I'm grateful that I was forced to pay attention to what matters—myself and my family—and had the courage to reassess my life.

Surround yourself with people who reflect who you want to be.

From that point, I was on a mission to build myself back up stronger from the inside out and teach others how to pay attention so they wouldn't make the same mistakes I did. I noticed how people were treating themselves and others in the workplace. I saw that by reframing conversations and actively listening, I could help people shift their mindsets and their moods. I was always talking with my network about the "people factor" and looking for leaders who "got it." Leaders who understood that people who have positive mindsets at work are more productive and engaged than those with negative mindsets. If revenue is king, then a positive mindset is the queen. They go hand in hand. Conversation after conversation, I talked about how investing in people would drive results, but I was usually met with blank stares and skeptics. After a while, I realized that I needed a new network.

I'm grateful that so many people didn't listen because it made me look beyond and challenged me to go further.

Good people know good people.

In early 2018, I saw a post on LinkedIn by Scott McGregor that mentioned growing up poor in the affluent town of Madison, Connecticut. Although I was not connected to him or anyone he was connected to, his post resonated with me because when I was growing up, my parents struggled financially. It also stood out because he lived in the next town over. I saw that he had started his own company, and since I had been thinking about leaving my job and starting my own company, I asked him to meet me for coffee.

I told him my story and why I wanted to jump into entrepreneurship to teach leaders how to take care of their biggest asset—their people. Scott said, "You have to do it. There is a desperate need for it. Companies are losing money every day because they don't have a strategy for hiring and retaining talent."

We clicked, and he asked me to write a chapter for the first book in the Standing O! series. He introduced me to amazing people who had also started businesses to fill unmet needs. To this day, I don't know how I saw that post. I believe that the timing was right and we were meant to meet. Oddly enough, I spent my entire career supporting people, believing in them, and giving them the courage to play bigger. Scott, who was a complete stranger, believed in me from that first meeting and inspired me to go after my dream and try something new.

I'm grateful that Scott was someone who shared my vision.

We rise by lifting others.

Soon after meeting Scott, I took the leap. I quit my corporate job and began pursuing a mission to bring people back into the conversation and be a voice for those who hadn't yet found their own. Scott and I joined forces because we realized we were better together and that high-growth startups need stronger strategies for hiring, onboarding, and retaining their people. I am exactly where I am meant to be, and I am grateful for every bump along the way because it led me here.

I'm grateful that my husband, kids, and extended family (my tribe) supported me in taking the scariest leap of my life.

When we look back, we discover it was never random. It is all connected.

My story is a small taste of what this book offers you, which is a peek into the lives of fifty-three incredible people. Our mission with the Standing O! book series is to give back and do something good. To be a ring in the ripple and inspire others to do the same. Remember, we don't need to look far for inspiration; it is right in front of us.

I hope that you use this book as a way to reflect on your journey and that it inspires you to own your story, see your strength, and have gratitude for who you are today.

I hope this book encourages you to look back and see that every situation teaches us something, makes us stronger, or helps us understand what we didn't see before.

Have gratitude for your journey.

Kirk Alemán is co-founder of DryErase Ventures, a venture capital firm focused on investing in underserved founders. He also serves as chief financial officer at United 4 Social Change, a nonprofit that creates civic leaders, and is currently a mentor at MassChallenge. He holds a master's degree in finance from Harvard University and has two pet guinea pigs named Bao Bao and Chun Chun.

. . . .

I'm the doctor who never was, and I'm okay with that.

When you come from an immigrant family, you're always told one thing: "You should grow up to be a doctor, a lawyer, or an engineer." Because of that mentality, I thought I wanted to be a doctor since I could first babble a few coherent words. I worked my tail off day in and day out through school to make sure that I achieved the goals necessary to get there, and soon enough, I was almost there. I was in medical school, but something was off.

I knew I could do it and make my family proud of me by giving them the satisfaction of saying, "That's my son: Doctor Alemán," but I felt like I was doing something more out of comfort than for happiness. Something had to change, and it turned out to be the hardest choice I've ever made: I dropped out of medical school.

As you can imagine, parents don't take news like their child dropping out of medical school very well, so my family was less than happy with me, to say the least. They were disappointed and worried about my future. But I kept reassuring them that everything was going to be all right, they just had to wait and see. There were moments when I doubted myself: Was I doing the right thing? Could I really succeed in a different career that wasn't what I had strived for my whole life?

The answers didn't come easily, and it took me a few years to figure out where

I was going. What I did know for sure, though, was that I wanted to prove to my parents that they could be proud of me even if I wasn't "Dr. Alemán."

I've tried it all: theater, photo shoots, retail, sales, marketing, and finance. It was a long process, and for awhile I couldn't figure out what I wanted to do, but I was fortunate enough that I could keep trying and not worry too much about the repercussions. Finally, I decided I needed a scene change. Having lived in New York City my whole life, I was in my comfort zone and needed to push past it. And then it happened. I got into Harvard and had a choice to make: Do I stay in New York City and try to make it work there, or do I take the leap and push past my comfort zone at home? I decided to say, "Whatever happens happens. Let's do it." Soon after, I moved to Cambridge, Massachusetts.

I can attribute that move to Cambridge as the catalyst for figuring myself out. Home was comfortable, but it was keeping me from pushing past whatever boundaries were holding me back. I started seeing things from a different perspective, almost as if through the eyes of a person who had the confidence of a seasoned veteran but the thirst of a man out to prove the naysayers wrong. I couldn't stop pursuing opportunity after opportunity, whatever the path, as long it was taking me in a positive direction.

I even co-founded a business—DryErase Ventures, a venture capital firm that invests in underserved founders who might otherwise be ignored by investors just because they aren't what others prototypically look for in a founder. I'm that unconventional founder, and I will always want to help others with a weird road like mine find their way.

Lifelong friends were found, big moves were made, fresh adventures started, and I'm sure exciting things still lie ahead. Am I scared every once in awhile? Sure. Worried that things won't work out? Heck no. Life is full of twists and turns, but I swear to you that it's worth it as long as you free yourself from the comfort of the known and embrace whatever lies beyond it.

I might not be the doctor my parents wanted, but I hope they are proud of the man I've become.

Darrell Amy

Darrell Amy is a trailblazer who is passionate about helping individuals, businesses, and nonprofits develop new ways to impact the world. He is the author of Revenue Growth Engine, a system to help 10,000 great businesses double revenue. He is a regular keynote speaker and co-host of the Selling From the Heart *podcast. In addition to being the founder of several businesses, he is co-chair of the Kingdom Missions Fund and executive director of the ManAlive EXPEDITION. Born in Canada, he now lives in the southern United States with his wife, three children, and a growing group of grandchildren. When not writing, speaking, or working, you can find him on his sailboat, camping, or hiking.*

. . . .

Rarely found in today's culture, faithfulness is a virtue of Paul Barber's that continues to inspire me. Over seven decades, he has demonstrated a steady faithfulness to his faith, his family, and his calling. This faithfulness has created a life of sterling integrity and powerful impact.

Paul discovered his passion for helping other people after he came to Christ during his college years. Shortly after graduating and marrying the love of his life, his love for others led him to a mission in Syracuse, New York, where he worked with inner-city kids.

After graduating, he accepted the call to build a missions training facility in Manila, Philippines. Moving to the other side of the planet, he gave up comfort and convenience to train others how to help people. Despite inconvenience, isolation, and intimidation from local authorities, Paul was faithful to the task before him. Through persistent faithfulness, he launched the first global training center for a movement that would impact people around the world.

Upon returning home to raise his family, Paul began a career in the business world. He worked faithfully for one company for his whole career, choosing to be a servant rather than bouncing around from job to job in pursuit of promotions and money.

While Paul was faithfully working in the business world, raising a family, and serving in his church, his passion for missions continued to grow. Moved by the fundraising letters he would receive from friends who were doing amazing work as missionaries, he would faithfully donate toward as many of these causes as he could. However, he always wanted to be able to give more.

Faithful to his passion, Paul began to dream about a better way to provide funds for these organizations. He thought that it might be possible to generate larger donations by creating an investment vehicle that gathered contributions from multiple businesses and individuals and then used the earnings from the investment to create an ongoing stream of funds for missions. He consulted with some financial advisors, but the idea hit several legal and tax roadblocks.

Faithfulness means not giving up. Paul held onto the vision for nearly a decade. Undeterred, he began saving $50 a month toward his vision, not knowing if it would come to pass.

When I met Paul, he was a leader in my church. One day, he asked me to go to Honduras to scout out a project where a school was being built to help educate street children from Tegucigalpa. With Paul's encouragement, I left my comfort zone and flew to Central America. What I saw on this trip changed my heart.

Several months after returning home, I was having lunch with Paul to get his input on a business plan I had crafted. The footnote to the plan referenced my intention to direct a percentage of the profits of the business to help missions organizations. Paul jumped on the idea.

Within a month, his faithfulness came to fruition when the Kingdom Missions Fund was born. Based on his $50-a-month savings and a big vision, the Kingdom Missions Fund has raised more than $700,000 to date and funded more than 200 grants for innovative missions projects around the world. The earnings from the fund's investments will provide a perpetual source of grants, allowing Paul's faithfulness to continue for decades to come.

Faithfulness continues to motivate Paul. As the Kingdom Missions Fund diversifies into micro loans, he recently traveled to the Democratic Republic of the Congo to explore ways to spur development inside impoverished communities. Undeterred by inconvenient travel, civil war, and a growing Ebola outbreak, he demonstrated a confident faithfulness that will undoubtedly lead to a project that will bring hope to many people who are currently feeling hopeless.

Paul's life has demonstrated the power of faithfulness. Even when times were tough and it seemed like nothing was happening, he remained faithful to his faith, his family, and his vision. As a result, not only has he lived a life of integrity, but his impact will go on for generations.

Ishveen Anand

Ishveen Anand is founder and CEO of OpenSponsorship.com, the largest sports sponsorship marketplace. It covers more than 150 sports and 5,500 professional athletes, teams, and events and has completed more than 3,000 deals. OpenSponsorship enables brands to optimize sports marketing campaigns with its software-enabled tools, including integrations with IBM Watson, Google Analytics, Shopify, and ROI tracking. A British native who graduated from Oxford University, Anand was on the Forbes 30 Under 30 2015 Sports list and has been featured in multiple publications as an expert on sports and influencer marketing. Prior to starting OpenSponsorship, she was a sports agent working with top teams, brands, and federations.

. . . .

My first meeting with the sports head of Hero MotoCorp (formerly Hero Honda) happened on a ridiculously hot and humid day in Delhi in May 2009. I was three months into living my new life as a sports agent in India after making the bold decision to leave a career at a management consultancy in London—a career that made a lot more sense given that I had studied economics and management at Oxford University.

I sat in the room with Mr. J. Narain as he lectured my boss and me about what he required for the upcoming ICC cricket tournament. With each demand, there was a lot of enthusiasm, and he was on the border of passionate and scary. I remember thinking that JN (as he is usually known) was a little too far into the weeds. Was there a need for so much micro detail? It was just a sports tournament after all!

Nonetheless, since I had landed in India, he was the first person who made me get out my laptop and put to work some of the consulting skills I'd formerly learned. That evening I went back to our office and put together a deck and various Excel files covering the deliverables he'd asked for with timelines, notes, cost analysis, and an array of other information that would be helpful to execute against his expectations. Two days later, I found out that JN had told my boss he wanted me to accompany him to England for the ICC T20 World Cup cricket tournament. JN said: "It's her plan. Let her deliver." Amazing—I was headed back home!

In June 2009, I was back in London four months after I'd left without knowing when I'd be back. I was ecstatic and couldn't wait to see my parents, sisters, friends, and former colleagues. Unfortunately, JN had other ideas. We sat together for eight-plus hours a day every day at each cricket match. For some of the matches, we had absolutely no work. We were just putting in face time—or as JN would say, we were observing and checking on the same deliverables again and again. During one match between two weaker teams, I asked him if I could come two hours late so I could have breakfast with my former vice president from my consulting days, to which JN said absolutely not. Suffice it to say, we didn't talk much when I got to the stadium.

After the one-month tournament, we returned to India, and I was definitely in a love/hate relationship with JN. We organized a debrief meeting a few days later, and after going through each item line by line, he turned to me and said, "Well, that's it. You passed." As if the entire tournament was a test. He said regardless of what happens from here on out, he would be there for me whenever I needed, adding, "You can call me your godfather." And just like that my client turned into one of the most influential figures in my life. It's one of the best things that has ever happened to me. Thank you, JN.

Here are the top three principles I have learned from you:

- Your work is your name. You are always accountable for what you hand in, so never deliver anything but the best.

- Lead by example. If you expect someone to be at a 6 a.m. meeting, make sure you're there five minutes before that, and they will follow.

- Expect perfection at all times so the people around you will either step up or filter out. Everyone wants to be surrounded by the best.

When people ask what it means to be an entrepreneur, I often say that it's like banging your head against a brick wall and knowing you need to break through. Today, I am able to have this mentality and face the impossible because JN taught me the art of persistence, sticking to the plan, expecting everyone around me and myself to step up when needed, and knowing that doing things even 80 percent is not acceptable. It wasn't easy having JN as a client, but having him as a godfather and a mentor made it worthwhile.

Kirat Anand founded and served as CEO of KAS New York, a women's contemporary ready-to-wear lifestyle brand whose clients included Neiman Marcus, Saks Fifth Avenue, Nordstrom, Bloomingdale's, and other top retailers. He has been featured in Entrepreneur *magazine,* Huffington Post, Elle, Glamour, *and others. He recently sold his company and currently serves as a board member, advisor, and mentor for a variety of organizations, including the New York University Leonard Stern School of Business's Fashion and Luxury MBA Council, Virgin Innovation Lab, and Stern Venture Fellows. Before becoming an entrepreneur, Anand was an investment banker at JPMorgan focused on technology, media, and telecommunications.*

. . . .

George Washington said, "My mother was the most beautiful woman I ever saw. All I am I owe to my mother. I attribute my success in life to the moral, intellectual, and physical education I received from her."

Growing up in Queens, New York, as the son of Indian Sikh immigrants wasn't easy. It was often rough and lonely, and there was a lot of social pressure to fit in. It didn't help that for the first twelve years of my life I was an only child. Not having any siblings or cousins I could turn to for guidance, advice, or comfort left me isolated and vulnerable.

Children need someone they can look up to, someone to help them get up after they've been knocked down. For me, that someone was my mother. She filled the role of the elder sibling, best friend, and eventually my mentor.

My mother gave birth to me when she was twenty-two, only a few years after she married my father and came to America. They were old-school entrepreneurs—Lin-Manuel Miranda might call them "young, scrappy, and hungry." Looking back, I can't imagine what they must have endured and sacrificed at such a young age to raise a child. They were all alone and starting a company in a foreign country with no family, friends, or financial support. And now they had the additional responsibility of raising a child. It didn't help that my father was traveling for work two hundred-plus days a year.

However, none of this fazed my mother. She was our rock and, most importantly, my source of strength and inspiration. If I had a science fair, music recital, or baseball practice, she was always there. She was there to see my electric conductor win second place at the science fair, cheered me on when I played the acoustic guitar in the school recital in fourth grade, and ran me through hours of baseball drills so I would be ready for my Little League games, which eventually led to me being a walk-on for the New York University baseball team.

Adolescent curiosity and the environment we grow up in affect what we believe and how we act, which becomes our reality and eventually defines who we are. By observing my mother's work ethic, optimistic demeanor, and devotion to spirituality, I can draw parallels to who I am today. These are the same characteristics that fuel my competitive fire. When I started KAS New York, all the naysayers lined up to say: "What does a former JPMorgan investment banker know about the women's fashion industry?" However, the work ethic, optimistic composure, and faith in myself that I learned from my mother helped me prevail.

When I was growing up, all my summer vacations were spent traveling overseas with my mother for her work engagements, visiting manufacturing facilities for sourcing and auditing. I would watch her teach pattern makers, seamstresses, and artisans how to cut and lay patterns, drape fabric, combine embroidery thread colors, and select prints. This exposure had a lasting effect on me and planted a designer seed in me that I wasn't even aware of at the time.

Those experiences nurtured my inner curiosity and passion to become a women's wear entrepreneur. Through my brand's journey, there was one main constant: my mentor, my partner, my rock—my mother.

Rob Anderson began his career as an athletic performance coach helping athletes improve their physical and mental health. Over the years, he has expanded his efforts and developed a series of training modules, courses, and programs that help athletes and athletic entrepreneurs reclaim their "why" and achieve accelerated success in their niche. His premier program, "Win by Design," provides a full program to help athletic-minded entrepreneurs get on track, get a clear focus, maximize their health, find their "why," find their edge, nail their message and purpose in the world, and run a business in alignment with their talents and values.

. . . .

I'm sure several people in *Standing O! Encore* have selected their parents as having had a profound impact on their lives.

If you take the next few minutes to read why my parents deserve a standing O, I'm confident this passage will enhance your perspective on life, parenting, and why the kitchen is the key to changing the world.

1. Faith

"You have a choice: Be part of the problem or part of the solution."

Those were my dad's words to me anytime I would start flipping out about not getting what I wanted, if I felt someone should have acted differently, or if I wanted a different result after an athletic contest.

Faith isn't about going to church or becoming a spiritual being, even though both of those things are important. A lot of people go to church or talk about being spiritual (non-church-goers) but don't EVER take action toward what they want in life or lean on their faith to help them create it.

Faith is about the action you take before your desires are created.

Hopefully, going to church or being spiritual gives you the confidence to take action and persevere through difficult times.

My dad's words have always been a powerful reminder that I can find a way through a challenge if I make the decision to be part of the solution. My faith gives me the courage to take action toward creating what I believe is possible by being part of the solution.

2. Fire

My dad has always been the voice of reason. He was a huge hulk of a man, with an even bigger presence. My dad was the type of person who didn't need to talk to be heard. My mom, however, is the FIRE!

She's a God-fearing woman who loves competition. She blessed my teammates by touching the hand of every player before the biggest games with a splash of holy water because she wanted everyone safe. But she also wanted everyone on our team to have the strength to annihilate our opponents.

These days, someone might want to sue the school for allowing that to happen or find a way to declare the players ineligible for recognizing a religious belief.

The main lesson I've learned from my mom is to question the rules—a lesson I've readily applied as a coach, a trainer, and a speaker to get results for people they may not otherwise have accomplished.

My mom doesn't know anything about lacrosse or football—the two sports that dominated my life as a kid. When she watches her grandkids compete in triathlons, basketball, gymnastics, or CrossFit, she doesn't know anything about the rules of those sports either.

But she knows how to share her passion. She isn't going to follow the "rules" of sitting quietly and clapping at the appropriate time. She's going to cheer if one of her grandkids delivers a big hit.

She's going to jump up and down after every score during a lopsided victory.

She's going to tell you how much she loved your celebration after you scored.

She's going to tell you that she loved how you showed your toughness and played after you were injured.

She's going to thank your coach for being tough on you.

She's going to buy you ice cream after the game—and a double scoop if you won.

In short, after watching my mom's reactions to sporting events all these years, I've learned to question the rules, push the limits, and walk an unorthodox path to achieving our desired results.

3. Kitchen

My greatest memories have always revolved around food. Breaking bread together as a team, as a trainer with my clients, as a father, as a friend, and as a husband has always created a stronger sense of unity within me and those attending the table.

When I was growing up, my parents always found a way to bring our home with us wherever we went. When I traveled with our church as a kid, we would eat homemade fried chicken and coconut bread as a group.

During our yearly family trips out of the county, one of my family members would make sandwiches, prepare snacks, or cut up fruit for our outings. When we would stop and eat together as a family, that small touch of home always gave me a sense of comfort.

Every program I've had the opportunity to lead or participate in as a player has had a routine of eating together every week—either at someone's home or during our film sessions. Those meals have always brought us closer together while creating memorable experiences.

If you want to change the world, bring your team together or unite your staff by breaking bread together. However, before you break bread, find out what they would like to eat.

If you don't know what they like for breakfast or whether they eat a light lunch—or if they're a vegetarian, vegan, or meat-eater—how can you ever expect them to:

- Buy into your mission?
- Support your agenda?
- Work when they're sick, injured, or tired?
- Give up time with their families?
- Stand by you when times are hard?

If you don't know how to feed the folks in your family or those working by your side, slow down and ask. They will pay you back by making a lifetime of sacrifices to serve the mission. If you want to change the world, figure out how to get everyone to the table and serve them a meal they will enjoy.

Thank you, Mom and Dad, for always feeding my mind, my body, and my spirit. Take a bow.

Ken Black's twenty-five-year career in and around Nike was built on changing the games of business and sport. His experience spans global creative direction of three Olympic Games, direction and launch of iconic brands and products such as Brand Jordan and Nike Free, and the startup of divisions such as Advanced Concepts and Nike Team Sports. He left Nike to help build the start-up SPARQ Training, which was later acquired by Nike (one-half) and ESPN (one-half). He has come to believe that "seeing different" is the secret to making companies, brands, products, or experiences that move people and now spends his time helping others do just that.

. . . .

Growing up through a twenty-five-year career at Nike fills me with gratitude for having been plugged directly into the power of sport.

One of the many examples of that power came on June 11, 1997. Three of us had just wrapped up meetings with the NFL in New York and were heading to the airport for our return flight to Portland, Oregon. As we were talking about our trip home, we realized our layover was in Salt Lake City, about three hours before the tipoff of game 5 of the NBA finals between the Chicago Bulls and their host, the Utah Jazz.

One of my teammates, Elliott Hill, acted quickly and placed a call to our NBA colleagues to see if there was any way to get tickets to that evening's game. Of course, text messaging didn't exist in 1997, so we had to wait until we landed in Salt Lake City to find out the answer. As you would expect in a story like this, Elliott had a message waiting when we landed that we did indeed have four tickets to the game at will call.

That night we witnessed, live, one of the greatest games in NBA history, now known as the Flu Game. On that night, Michael Jordan won a courageous battle over a flu bug and willed himself to a thirty-eight-point performance, hitting the game-winning shot and leading the Bulls to a 90-88 win over the Jazz. This gave Chicago a 3-2 game lead that they never relinquished as they went on to win another title.

The power of sport on display? Most definitely I felt it. But another story that night showed the real power of sport.

Once we knew we had the tickets waiting for us, we had to convince Delta to extend our layover overnight. At the Delta help desk, Elliott explained the situation to a flight attendant and added, "We have four tickets to tonight's game, but there are only three of us so we'd be happy for you to have that fourth ticket if you can help us extend our stay in SLC." Her eyes lit up and she asked, "Can I give that ticket to someone else?"

We found ourselves before the game in front of the Delta Center with our accomplice and her sixteen-year-old son, Tim. She was excited for him to experience the game and had given him her ticket.

As the game began, Elliott asked Tim if his dad took him to many Jazz games, to which Tim replied, "My dad died last month."

Of course, at this point, we ratcheted up the experience for Tim, flooding him with food and drink and pictures of him by the court. The game changed for us right there, and it became about Tim's experience that night.

When we returned to the front of the Delta Center after the game and brought Tim back to his mom, he hustled over and gave her a tremendous hug. His back was to us, but we could see her face and the tears that began streaming down her cheeks. After the hug, I pulled Tim away for a moment to say goodbye and so that Elliott could ask his mom how she was doing. She replied, "He just thanked me and told me he loved me. His dad was his best friend, and he hasn't spoken since he passed away." I keep the ticket to that game not for the memory of Michael Jordan's performance but as a reminder of the REAL story of that night.

My standing O is for Elliott Hill for teaching me that seeing opportunity, seizing it, and exhibiting gratitude for what you receive and generosity for what you can give will create possibilities for connecting people and creating incredible, life-changing stories.

Lindsey Boggs is a social selling evangelist and leader who has traveled the world teaching the ways of modern-day selling. Because of her articles about the techniques of prospecting with LinkedIn and her social presence, she has shared the stage with many icons and become a TEDx speaker. She loves to teach and have an impact on people's lives with her passion for sales.

. . . .

James Copley changed my life. Without him, I would not be where I am today.

When I was hired straight from college for my first "real-world" job at FedEx Office corporate in Dallas, I never imagined James would have such an impact on my life. My college degree was in classical music, so I had no idea what I was getting myself into by going into business.

They hired me as an executive assistant. I expected my life to be like the movie The Devil Wears Prada, and by some, I was treated that way. By others, like James, I was not.

James treated me like an equal, and I looked up to him so much. Instead of blowing me off when I asked questions about the company's strategy, he took the time to explain it to me. He was also able to balance a very demanding role while having a great quality of life at home, which was something I wanted to have in my own life. I'll never forget emailing him one night about work, and he emailed me back and told me to stop working.

James not only had an impact on my professional life, but my personal life as well. I'll always remember him saying not to be "house poor." My husband and I often talk about upgrading our house, and I hear that voice in my head saying not to be house poor.

After I was promoted from James' team to another, we still kept in touch—daily, in fact. I would get to work early like he did (well, not 5 a.m. early like he did!) and share our morning updates. I also became close with his entire family, and to this day, we still talk at least once a week, sometimes more.

When I got into sales, he was so proud of my success. He knew I wanted to do more with my life, and he has continued to be supportive and encourage me in my career. Whenever we get a chance to schedule business trips in the same city, we take advantage of it because he now lives in Arizona and I live in North Carolina.

When I think about key people who have had an impact on my life, my first thought is of James. He would do anything for me, and he is always willing to go the extra mile to help someone out.

Thank you, James, for always being my number-one fan and for pushing me hard. Thank you for educating me about business, teaching me about growing up, and hiring me when I lied about knowing Excel. You will always be a wonderful friend and mentor.

Tiffani Bova has been included among the top 50 sales and marketing influencers by Top Sales *magazine and has most recently been named a thinker of the month by Thinkers50 and one of the most powerful and influential women in California by the National Diversity Council. Her book,* Growth IQ, *was designated one of the top five leadership and strategy books in 2018 by 800-CEO-READ and was a Wall Street Journal bestseller. She has given over 500 keynote speeches on sales transformation and contributed to publications such as* Harvard Business Review, Forbes, *and* Entrepreneur. *Her* What's NEXT! *podcast has quickly become a top sales podcast, according to* Top Sales *magazine.*

. . . .

My mom, Dolors Judd, was a schoolteacher, and my dad was a banker, so we were the classic middle-class family living in Hawaii. They divorced when I was very young, and Mom became a single parent of a very active, sports-oriented child. I played everything I could and learned to win with humility, lose with my head held high, be coachable, and contribute to a team.

Mom had a selfless devotion and embodied pure, unadulterated chutzpah. She demonstrated perseverance and a strong work ethic by teaching during her breaks to ensure I wanted for nothing. Above all, she was fiercely independent. Smart in so many ways, she always made me feel I could make decisions on my own, good or bad, and course-correct because of the years I spent watching her do it.

Her dad was more than a grandfather to me. He visited often, and I traveled much of the world with him before the age of fifteen. In Hawaii, a true melting pot of the Asia Pacific region, I was blonde, green-eyed, and fair-skinned and one of the only Caucasian children in preschool. I was exposed to many different cultures, which gave me a very open, diverse lens on the world that impacts my ability to understand and embrace different cultures today.

In high school, my best friend's mother, Linda Fernandez, was president of EK Fernandez Shows and Fernandez Fun Factory, a carnival and indoor arcade business in Hawaii that had been family-run since 1903. While I was a freshman in high school, I worked at the outdoor games at the carnival unpacking teddy bears, managing the crew, setting up the trailers, marketing, handing out scripts, counting cash from 9 a.m. to midnight, and restocking for the next day until three in the morning. Sometimes we would have to sleep in the teddy bear trailers for two and a half days because there wasn't enough time to go home, sleep, and get back. Then we'd shut down, move to another location, and do it all again the following weekend while I attended class during the week. It was the hardest I think I have ever worked.

Everything I learned about business I learned at the carnival: supply chain by getting the teddy bears delivered on time, cost of goods on the plush, staffing choices, and light profit and loss by counting the cash and understanding what was needed to remain profitable. Linda was one of the first women in the Young Presidents Organization in Hawaii, and I wanted to grow up to be like her—the CEO of my own multimillion-dollar company.

I worked with Linda all through high school and after college, when I opened the biggest flagship store for The Fun Factory in Maui. She had the roof built to resemble a big-top tent, with a bowed ceiling lit by over 10,000 light bulbs. She and my mom flew in for the grand opening, and I wanted to impress them both. I was excited when I saw Linda arrive, shaking hands with everyone. She stopped in front of me and pointed her finger up to the sky without saying a word, and my eyes followed her gaze. One light bulb was burned out.

Over 15,000 square feet of organized accomplishment and the one broken lightbulb was what she spotted. That single moment shaped my view of the customer experience: All this can be right and one thing can be wrong, and people will remember that one thing. Our brand was the ultimate customer experience.

Thirty years later, when I spot a sign with a missing letter, I think to myself, "Linda would fire you!" Customer experience is the sum of every touch point you have. Ironically, my college counselor thought business was not for me, yet my real-life experience working for Linda showed me otherwise. She was committed to transferring knowledge to me in a way that shaped who I am professionally, and I always reflect on that story.

Everyone wants to go to Hawaii; it's a dream place with an Aloha spirit. Now I work for Salesforce, and I'm fortunate to be part of the Salesforce Ohana, a deep-seated support system we nurture inside the company with our employees, partners, customers, and members of the communities we call home. Joining Salesforce was a full-circle moment for me.

I often quote "Trust the process," and I live it every day. It ultimately led me to my current path and back to my roots. I may not need to sleep in the teddy bear trailers anymore, but I find myself hanging out with all the Salesforce mascots, Astro and Friends, just like my carnival days.

David Cancel

David Cancel is founder and CEO of Drift, the world's leading conversational marketing and sales platform. After just two years, the company was named to the Forbes Cloud 100, LinkedIn Top 50 Startups, Entrepreneur's Top Company Cultures, Boston Business Journal's Best Places to Work, and SaaS Company of the Year by the New England Venture Capital Association. Cancel is also known for creating hypergrowth products and product teams at companies such as HubSpot, Performable, Ghostery, and Compete. He has been featured in The New York Times, Forbes, Fortune, Wired, *and* Fast Company *and has guest lectured on entrepreneurship at Harvard Business School, MIT's Sloan School of Management, and other universities.*

. . . .

My mom, Cecilia, was a single mother who raised two of us boys. She was from Ecuador and didn't speak English well. In some ways, I feel she sacrificed at least her adult life for my brother and me because she worked seven days per week to support us. As hard as things may get for me at times, I look back to my mother's dedication and think I haven't worked a week in my life as hard as she has.

My mother's motto was: "The lazy person does twice the work"— meaning that when you are lazy about doing something, you will end up having to spend more time and energy to do it right later. Anytime I have ever tried to take a shortcut or quickly do something, I end up doing it over, and I can hear her saying that to me.

It's taken me most of my adult life to learn to apply the things she taught me. Some were about small and funny things, but many were life lessons about people and character. It took me nearly twenty years professionally to figure out what we all know now: You become the average of the people around you. She had been telling me that forever, but I didn't really listen.

These lessons crystallized for me after I started my first company, when

I was reflecting and looking back. I loved everything about it, but I had not created the culture I wanted because I was never intentional about it. I was intentional about the products, services, and customers but not when it came to hiring people for a cultural fit. From that point forward, I was committed to making culture the most important thing, and every company I have started since has gotten better. Drift is the most intentional I have ever been when it comes to hiring people and deciding who we surround ourselves with as an organization, so much so that it has become an internal leadership principle we hold dear.

Once I had my own kids, I noticed how much they watch and model me. My daughter is fourteen now, and at times, I feel like she can see right through me. She knows if I am in a bad mood or if something is wrong with me, even if I put on a good face. I reflect on my mom and realize that I absorbed specific lessons from her, although she may never have verbalized them. She demonstrated them to me by the way she carried herself. I don't know why it takes so long to learn these basic lessons in life; perhaps they are so obvious we ignore them.

Charlie Munger said: "I constantly see people rise in life who are not the smartest, sometimes not even the most diligent, but they are learning machines. They go to bed every night a little wiser than they were when they got up, and boy, does that help, particularly when you have a long run ahead of you."

Becoming a "learning machine" is core to myself and my company, and I owe a debt of gratitude to my mother for instilling in me the values and competencies that I bring into everything I do.

Tabitha Cavanagh

Tabitha Cavanagh is vice president of SomethingNew LLC and a positive disruption ambassador. She is also a Never Too Young Advisory Board co-chair and creator of #StrongAssMindset. She is a young-onset advocate, patient ally, and colon cancer thriver. She regained her life and found her voice after an unexpected cancer diagnosis at a young age. Life post-cancer led her to the field of recruiting, where she discovered her passion to help the right people come together for the right opportunities at the right time. Dedicated to assisting others in developing meaningful and intentional mindsets, she believes we can do anything our minds say we can.

. . . .

We only sell ourselves short when we are convinced we have no choice in our solution. It might not seem like there's much of a choice in a cancer diagnosis, but there is!

Out of nowhere, cancer bravely chose me. I was thirty-one years old and newly married with a toddler at home. Cancer didn't care. But I did. Cancer picked the wrong girl.

When I first heard the words: "You have stage III colon cancer," my boat was rocked in a big way. I was facing the scariest of unknowns. Amid the unexpected whirlwind, I immediately knew that I would have to take risks, make decisions without regret, and fight for my life. While I most definitely did not choose cancer, what I did choose was positivity and a #StrongAssMindset.

My first standing O goes out to the man who saved my life: Dr. Thomas Garofalo, a colorectal surgeon at the Cleveland Clinic. After getting multiple opinions from doctors who weren't sure what to do, Dr. Garofalo was the first to identify and explain a clear plan of action with confidence. Resolute despite previous medical opinions, he moved forward with speed, determination, and grace. He had the unique ability to make life-altering decisions in an instant and did so without pause.

When he couldn't successfully execute his initial plan, he was able to adapt on the fly to pull off a miracle. He made saying goodbye to eight inches of my colon an easy process. He is 100 percent one of my angels!

During my cancer journey, on the most difficult of days, I had to choose to see the sunshine. I spent the better part of a year physically struggling, but I decided to be thankful every morning before my feet even hit the floor. I started my days running toward gratitude. I found that choosing to see my cancer as a blessing truly helped it become one. In the blink of an eye, I realized my mindset was everything. My body could do *anything* my mind said it could. I believe this was the first time I ever saw something terrible as a gift.

Cancer taught me that people show up. I experienced an outpouring of love, supporting the notion that "cancer requires community." My family, friends, and strangers who became family reached out to care for me in ways I could never have imagined. I will forever be grateful to those who showed up and gave so much of themselves when I could provide very little in return. I strive daily to "repay" the efforts of many. To my husband, my daughter, my family, my friends, and my cancer community: Thank you! Thank you from the bottom of my butt!

You might not know what to say when someone tells you they have cancer, but try anyway. Your words don't need to be "perfect." Show them love. Show them kindness. Show them grace. No one should have to battle this alone.

Cancer taught me to make the most of my minutes. Looking forward to something in the future was simply me exercising my imagination. What was even better than that was living intentionally in each moment as it presented itself.

From chemo treatments to various surgeries to how I spent my good days, I took everything one moment at a time. I stopped waiting for life to happen and started creating it instead. I didn't come this far to only go this far.

We all have minutes. They aren't the same, but we do hold the power to use those minutes however we please.

This moment, *right now*, is your only guaranteed moment today. We don't know what else the day will bring. Are you spending your minutes doing the things that feed your soul and bring you joy?

There are a million ways to make the most of your minutes. It's going to look different for everyone. Whatever that means for you, find it and then go do the damn thing.

There's no perfect progression. I'm better because of the mountains I've climbed. I've embraced my challenges and have even learned to let them excite me.

I've learned to show up, live on purpose, and exceed my own expectations. At first, I was surprised by what I was capable of. Then I came to expect that kind of greatness from myself. I dug deep and discovered my unknown grit and unconditional gratitude. We don't always get to choose what happens to us, but we can choose what we do with it. I chose the journey. I chose to rise up. I chose to regain my life.

The fact that you might be struggling right now doesn't make you a burden. It doesn't make you "less than." It makes you qualified. Qualified to turn your chaos into a blessing. Qualified to find your voice. Qualified to help others, and qualified to regain your life. Love where you are right now, and if you need to, choose to flip your narrative.

Remember that at any given time, you are where you're needed. Your story is unfolding. You can choose to climb out and rise through the mud or let it swallow you whole. It's like anything else you want to get better at. You must first embrace the change. An open mind is the perfect breeding ground for growth.

So cheers to you, Dr. Garofalo. Because of you, I have a second chance to live my best life. I'm able to continue fighting in honor of those who can't. Because of you, I'm still here to use my story of survival for good. I promise to never again take my life for granted. You've given me the greatest gift, and because of you, I'm able to watch my daughter grow up.

Thank you, thank you, thank you!

Create a life you love. Believe in you, and don't you dare wait for permission.

Perspective takes practice and patience. My hope is that you will rise up. My hope is that you will run toward gratitude. My hope is that you will always remember you, too, can do hard things.

I promise *the journey is worth it.*

As Erma Bombeck said: "When I stand before God at the end of my life, I would hope that I would not have a single bit of talent left and could say, 'I used everything you gave me.'"

Sharon Cirillo

Sharon Cirillo is a ghost writer and content creator at DSE Communications. With over a decade in financial services and as many years as a small-business owner, she draws on real-life, corporate, and entrepreneurial experience when composing material for clients. Her expertise is in helping others express themselves and convey their voice via ghost writing, blog posts, articles, editorials, and copy for sales and marketing collateral. She is a contributor to Thrive Global, a Huffington Post *property, and has her own blog titled Perfectly Imperfect.*

. . . .

When I was asked to contribute a chapter to this wonderful book, I knew immediately that I would write about my beautiful niece, Kate Cirillo-Rice.

Born to my brother Gregory and his wife, Carole, Katie was their only child and an amazing kid. Always smiling, loving, and caring, she grew up to be a very wise old soul, touching everyone she met. In the early years, we were all quite close and lived in the same town. Shortly after we lost our mother, they moved a few hours south to be near Carole's parents. Although we still saw each other on occasion, it was Facebook that kept me abreast of most things. As a newly divorced single mother, I was in a state of "surviving not thriving" and in my own little world. The time passed quickly.

One Mother's Day morning, my phone rang, and my brother said Kate was having some abdominal pain. They had just returned from vacation, and although she seemed a bit tired, everything else appeared normal. Although we weren't happy about her having to be seen by a doctor, no one expected what followed.

It was after 8 p.m. when he finally called me back. Through painful tears, he described the X-rays and CT scans that showed masses throughout her abdomen with the largest on her colon, which was causing her pain. Time stood still. There was no air left to breathe. What ensued was a battery of tests from the top cancer center in our area, ending with a diagnosis of stage IV cancer and minimal treatment options. This beautiful, healthy twenty-five-year-old girl was terminally ill.

When things like this happen, suddenly nothing else matters. I got in my car and drove to their house. When I arrived, I awkwardly approached her, feeling more like a stranger than family. I looked into her huge blue eyes and said, "I am so sorry, Katie. I am sorry for letting things come between your dad and me and missing out on your life as a result." I could barely get the words out because I was crying so hard.

She grabbed my hand and said, "It's okay, Aunt Sharon, you are here now." At that moment, I felt every drop of remorse, confusion, and resentment drain from my body. We were family.

I spent nearly every weekend between May and September at their house, with weekday visits when I could take off from work. My life ran on auto-pilot, and my kids and job survived it. We talked about deep and meaningful things. We discussed the madness of our family, the ridiculousness of life, and the absurdity of not burning the Yankee candles because we were "saving them." Katie and her longtime boyfriend, Bruce, had talked about marriage and having a family, and she still dreamed of "saying yes to the dress."

Not once did I see her cry. She said she cried when no one else was around because she didn't want to make them feel any worse than they already did. She was more worried about her parents and Bruce than herself. Bruce never left her side, and in July, she tried an experimental treatment that didn't work. Week after week passed, and I could tell she was getting worse.

At that point, I asked her if she was still comfortable having an "extra person" like me around so often. I wanted to be sure she had privacy when she didn't feel well. She just held my hand and said, "You aren't an extra person. I'm happy when you are here." I am not sure I had ever felt such love and acceptance.

Bruce surprised her by finding a justice of the peace and quickly organizing a wedding. He carefully and lovingly washed her hair, did his best to put some makeup on her, and purchased a beautiful white dress for her to wear. My brother wheeled her down a makeshift aisle in their living room, and although it wasn't the wedding anyone had pictured, she became Mrs. Bruce Rice. She died shortly after.

I have a photo on my phone of her delicate hand atop his, clad with family heirloom ruby rings, to remind me of the ripple of selflessness I experienced during that period. Bruce was selfless to Katie, and Katie was selfless to everyone, especially me. She could have greeted me in May with an attitude or a cordial but semi-aloof demeanor for not having been around much. Instead, she allowed me back into her life as if I had never left it.

She not only demonstrated the act of forgiveness, but she offered the gift of reconciliation, and it changed me.

A happy-go-lucky kind of girl, she always imparted light-hearted wisdom, and I pass some of it on to you:

- Lighten up. What's bothering you probably doesn't matter.

- Course-correct quickly. Not everyone you love will still want to be there once you figure your crap out.

- Listen to music all the time because it cleanses the soul and lifts your spirits.

- Say "I love you" even if you don't hear it back.

- Don't shut people out even if they did it to you. Let them in.

- Take naps in the sun. Yes, you have time.

- Adopt and love a dog. It will change your life for the better.

- Dream big.
-
- Don't go to bed angry.

- Watch comedy before you fall asleep—and never, ever the news.

- You take your trash to the curb for a reason. Leave it there.

- Believe in angels. Believe in mermaids, too.

- Bravery lives inside each of us; we just don't know it at times.

- Whenever possible, make peace and make things right.

- Not everyone can forgive you, and it will hurt. Accept it and stay loving anyway.

- Don't settle. Ever.

- Laugh until your face hurts sometimes.

Katie, this standing O is for you.

Daniel Disney

Daniel Disney is one of the world's leading sales and social selling experts. With an audience of more than 500,000 followers, his sales blog and other content reach millions of salespeople every month. He travels the world speaking at events and training salespeople how to leverage LinkedIn and social selling to their full potential alongside (not instead of) traditional sales methods. He is the founder and owner of The Daily Sales, LinkedIn's most popular page for salespeople.

. . . .

When I was invited to contribute to this amazing book and give a standing ovation to someone important, one person came right to the front of my mind—someone who was quite possibly one of the biggest influences on my career and life, someone who inspired me to work in sales, and someone who guided me to be the best I could possibly be.

This person is someone I very rarely speak about because, unfortunately, I lost him just over four years ago. This person is my Uncle Al.

Uncle Al was a huge part of our family. He was the husband of my mother's sister and always the center of attention. Full of personality, energy, and love, he was always there for all of us. Uncle Al had a hugely inspiring sales career and spent years managing key accounts at British Airways then leading sales teams in the luxury retirement sector.

Ever since I was very young, Uncle Al told me that he knew I would be successful. It was nice to hear, but I never understood what it was that I would be successful in. Although he never pushed me to go into sales, I think he knew it was something I would enjoy a lot.

When I was sixteen years old, I got my very first job—at Homebase, a UK-based do-it-yourself store, on the checkouts. After a few weeks, I was offered a promotion into the sales department. I phoned Uncle Al, and he told me to do what I felt I would enjoy. Having followed his career in sales, I knew this was something I wanted to do.

To celebrate, Uncle Al took me out to buy me my very first suit. Through the years, he was one of the biggest influences in my sales career, guiding me to listen more than talk, make my customers feel valued, solve problems, and be persistent. He taught me everything he knew.

Every time I saw him, he would sit me down and ask me loads of questions about the sales I had won, the sales I had lost, and the sales I was working on. He would then tell me about his, and together we would learn. I got to see early on just how rewarding a career in sales could be. While I was working hard at the start of my career, Uncle Al was enjoying the fruits of a long, successful career. He and my aunt traveled the world, had a beautiful house, and enjoyed the finer things in life. When we all went out for meals, it was always Uncle Al's treat.

Uncle Al put everything into his career, but unfortunately, after many successful years, the company he worked for fell into trouble, and as a result, Uncle Al, along with many others, was made redundant. He lost the job he loved.

It was out of the blue, and the shock hit Uncle Al hard. He had worked so hard and achieved so much that I don't think he ever expected something like this. The shock caused an immense amount of stress and led to health issues. Unfortunately, he didn't make it through them.

Uncle Al didn't get to see me launch The Daily Sales, and he never saw me become a keynote speaker and trainer. He didn't get to see me named one of the most influential people in the world in sales over the past two years. Every day I hope that if he had, I would have made him proud.

I didn't get to connect with Uncle Al on LinkedIn, but I found his profile and this recommendation that summed him up perfectly: "Alan is an inspirational, charismatic, generous born leader who brings all in his path along with him. Coaching, mentoring, and guiding direct reports and peers alike with huge aplomb and success. A sales and marketing guru who will no doubt accelerate his career."

My standing O is to my Uncle Al, the man who inspired me to sell and taught me how to do it well. Not a day goes by that I don't think of you, and I'm doing my very best to help inspire as many people in sales as I can, the same way you inspired me.

Jake Dunlap designs repeatable, sustainable sales models and processes that outperform industry standards. As the founder and CEO of Skaled Consulting, he helps executives around the world accelerate business growth with data-backed sales solutions. Before building Skaled, he held the roles of vice president of sales at Nowait (acquired by Yelp), head of sales and customer success at Chartbeat, and vice president of sales at Glassdoor (acquired by Recruit Holdings for $1.2 billion in 2018).

. . . .

Evan Ross was my first leader and mentor after I left sports. In the sports industry, I was confident and a high performer, and I felt as though I had a lot of natural talent from a sales perspective. During my time with the Tampa Bay Rays and Arizona Coyotes, I worked with great leaders, but they didn't really help me understand the bigger picture—how sales could be a career and not just a job.

Evan taught me two things in the first two months I worked with him, and he wasn't even my direct boss. He was my boss's boss and director of sales at CareerBuilder. But in just a couple of critical conversations I had with him, he shaped the rest of my career.

The first thing he taught me—in my first month with the company—was how to use a sales process. Sounds pretty simple for a sales guy, right? Only if you do it.

I had studied a lot of books, but I didn't really have a sales process or system that I used or brought with me from my previous roles. So when I started my first job outside the sports world, I really struggled. A month in, I had a conversation with Evan and wondered why a bunch of people in my training class had already started closing deals while I had yet to close one. Evan took the time to listen to one of my sales calls and afterward asked why I wasn't following the process they had taught me. I didn't have an answer. He then said to me, "Jake, do you think we trained 1,000-plus people on this process because it doesn't work?"

This was a revelation for me. I put the process in place the next month, and I crushed it. I closed $60,000 in new business that month. It was the first time I thought, "Wow, sales is a process as much as it is a science."

The second thing Evan taught me was how to set goals. Most people think goals are bars that you set and try to climb toward, but he helped me understand the importance of setting very specific goals during another conversation we had in my early days at CareerBuilder.

We had a meeting about my future at the company, and he asked me what my goals were and what I wanted to do. I said I wanted to be in leadership. He then said something I'll never forget: "That's not a goal, Jake." Boom. Mind blown.

Naturally, the next thing I said was of course leadership is a goal. He told me it's not a goal because I can't control it. He controls whether he promotes me or not. So what could I control? The answer was my activity—the work I put in and whether I was being a good team member, following best practices, and hitting my numbers. But more importantly, was I already leading the team even though that wasn't my role yet? Was I training and mentoring people?

This was the second time in two months that Evan had effectively changed my career. I truly understood goal setting and how to hit those goals. I didn't overthink it. I just did it. And I was promoted to a leadership role in my first three months at the company.

In a short period of time, Evan taught me two very important things that set me up for the rest of my career: 1) understanding the importance of following a process and 2) knowing that goals must be tangible and things that I can control. He also indirectly taught me a third thing: "Managing up" is as simple as asking your manager what his or her expectations are for you.

I can't send enough good vibes Evan's way for giving me these career and life lessons that I've been able to take with me from my first position as a vice president of sales to my current role as a CEO, where I try to instill and pass these lessons along to my own team.

So a big thanks to you, Evan. More good vibes coming your way.

Nicholas Elmi

After winning season 11 of Bravo's Top Chef, *Nicholas Elmi left the renowned Le Bec-Fin to open his first restaurant, Laurel, which was named one of the best new restaurants in America by the James Beard Foundation and one of the ten best restaurants in the country by* GQ. *Elmi followed up with a contemporary cocktail bar next door to Laurel named In the Valley. In 2017, determined to bring casual French cuisine to a wider audience, he introduced Royal Boucherie in Old City, Philadelphia. This fall, he will release his first cookbook,* Laurel: Modern American Flavors in Philadelphia, *with co-author Adam Erace.*

. . . .

When I look back on the various moments of my childhood, my mind rarely wanders down roads of sadness. Memories like these are good and vivid: waking up in the bed of my father's pickup truck on Sunday mornings and begging him to take us—me, my sister, and my brother—to get chocolate chip pancakes after he finished delivering papers. We'd laugh as we bounced around and played games on top of the giant stacks of bundled newspapers. Dad would peek his head in once every half-hour or so to restock the front seat. The three of us admired how quickly he would fold, elastic, and throw a paper that seemed to land exactly where he wanted it to almost rhythmically every time.

Dad would wake up early and deliver papers, then come home and have breakfast with us only to zip off to his real job working for Hewlett-Packard or the Eagle-Tribune or a vending machine company. I'm not really sure. I remember the way we'd poke fun at my mom as she got dressed in a bonnet and a lace apron for her night job serving mediocre American food at a high-end restaurant because being a teacher for mentally disabled children didn't exactly cut it financially when you had a family to support. We moved around a lot, but we always saw it as an adventure.

Slices of life in my memory take me back to the first day in a new house, dividing up the bedrooms, deciding who got what bathroom and who had to bunk with whom, and then doing it all over again a year later. From rental house to rental house, we were always excited to meet new friends, find new paths, and enroll in new schools. Mom would teach during the day, run us from school to practice to home, and then zoom off again to work for the night. On the nights she wasn't working, we'd sit down to dinner at 6:30. Together. Eventually she became a hostess at a Caribbean restaurant where she worked nights and weekends while still teaching on the outskirts of the city during the week.

We would water ski a lot. My father competed in weekend tournaments all along the East Coast. We'd travel together in a Suburban or one of those station wagons with the wood paneling on the side. We'd camp out at the tournament site and sleep in a tent together. My brother and I would bring our bikes so we could explore the towns, looking for new kids to play with or candy stores to visit. Sometimes, if my parents were doing well, we would stay in a hotel or a lake house. However, I always preferred sleeping in tents. It was exciting to make hand puppets on the tent's nylon roof using flashlights to cast shadows for our characters. We'd wake at dawn to the sound of a boat in the water and feel the cold dew of the grass between our toes as we'd step out of the tent for the first time that day. Often, we forgot where we were.

On those Sunday rides home, we'd sit in the back of the station wagon and eat penny candy from Cumberland Farms and shoot finger guns at other motorists. When we'd wake up for school on Monday mornings, Dad would be just coming back from another early morning paper route, cracking jokes and kissing Mom.

As we got older, my brother, sister, and I got a variety of jobs at restaurants around town, bussing and food running. I wasn't very good at being a food runner. Or a busboy. Or basically any job where I had to interact with a customer. Management quickly picked up on my character flaw, and I got a job washing dishes at an Italian trattoria—away from the public's eye. I loved the place. All the pasta was made on site, as were the pastries, and the restaurant was run by a family and a chef who was stern but sweet. One day, the pasta cook didn't show up for work. I was the only extra set of hands, so I stepped up.

I discovered two things in that moment: first, that all my vast and assorted childhood experiences had shaped me and formed my character, and second, that my character was solid and I would strive for excellence in everything I would do going forward. Today, I have a beautiful family of my own, and I own several award-winning restaurants.

Being a chef is not an easy gig. Long hours. Long weeks. Slim margins. And more often than not, the work is chaotic and desperate behind the scenes—cooks not showing up, pipes bursting in the basement, gas leaks in the building next door. But through it all, I have the steadfast determination of my parents to make my customers and my team feel welcomed, loved, and appreciated. I owe my ability to dampen the struggle and highlight the joys to my parents, who did that for me.

Dave Gerhardt

Dave Gerhardt is vice president of marketing at Drift. He started as a senior marketing manager in 2015 and was the company's first full-time marketing hire. He helped Drift grow its revenue from $0 to eight-plus figures and become one of the fastest-growing software-as-a-service companies. He is co-author of the bestselling book Conversational Marketing *with Drift CEO David Cancel and co-creator of the HYPERGROWTH business event, which will reach 10,000 people in Boston, San Francisco, and London in 2019. He is the host of the* Marketing Swipe File *podcast and co-host of the* Seeking Wisdom *podcast and was named Comparably's Top Marketing Leader for 2019.*

. . . .

The person who's had the most significant impact on my life and career is David Cancel, founder and CEO of Drift. Working for David for the past four years has taught me the skills and principles to set me up in my career forever, and they go beyond marketing. He has helped me learn how to be the next best version of myself every day.

He frequently talks about adopting and understanding the power of learning, specifically as it relates to investing in one's self. I've always done the outer work of taking care of my health and eating right, but for the first twenty-eight years of my life, I didn't like reading books and hadn't done much to strengthen my mind.

One day, David said to me, "Hey, you love marketing. Go read books about that." The next thing I knew, he was feeding me classic marketing books, such as *Ogilvy on Advertising, Cashvertising, Breakthrough Advertising, Positioning* by Al Ries and Jack Trout, and *The 22 Immutable Laws of Marketing,* to name a few—all books that were still relevant years after they were first published. I soaked it all in and applied the lessons learned in the books to our business at Drift. Seeing the principles firsthand opened my eyes to just how much a person can learn.

David is also a big believer in the "abundance mindset." So many people think: "Why spend $12 on a book that I might not even read?" and they talk themselves out of it. But that same person will spend that amount of money on coffee at Starbucks, which only benefits them for a short period. The abundance mindset is a shift in perspective, one that makes learning a priority. The great thing about your mindset is that it's very much within your control, and if you can harness it and apply it to learning, it can change your life.

Jim Rohn said, "Leaders are readers," and it's true. When you look at the best people in business and in life, like David Cancel, they are always growing and absorbing. In fact, we started a podcast together a few years ago titled *Seeking Wisdom*, and one of the first episodes we did was called "Secrets to Becoming a Learning Machine." That got me excited about becoming a learning machine and making sure I applied all that I gained every single day.

Another life-changing lesson I learned from David is to focus on people from all walks of life. The power of social psychology is that if you can understand how people think and how the mind works, you can be impactful. He taught me to understand the twenty-five cognitive biases people have and their differences in thinking, and he recommended books such as *Influence* by Robert Cialdini; *Thinking, Fast and Slow* by Daniel Kahneman; and *Predictably Irrational* by Dan Ariely. These have all been hugely impactful to my career in sales, marketing in business, and life.

Every minute, every day, every week, every month, and every year, we face new technology and trends, and things keep changing at a rapid pace. It's challenging to figure out what to keep up with and what's worth paying attention to, but those are the easy things to learn. People are harder to understand, but if you read a book from the 1700s or 1800s, you will realize that people have not changed. We all have the same desires, wants, and emotions that we've had since we were initially created. In life and business, if you can understand how people act and think, you can help them make better decisions. You will be a better person because of it and gain clarity about yourself.

Now that I know the biases that I may have and the way our brains work, I've become a better thinker and more effective in decision-making, hiring, leadership, training, and relationships. David taught me to focus on people and figure out the rest.

Kara Goldin

Kara Goldin is founder and CEO of Hint Inc., which produces flavored water with no added sweeteners or preservatives. She has received numerous awards, including being named to Fast Company's list of the most creative people in business, Fortune's most powerful women entrepreneurs, Forbes' 40 women to watch over 40, and the Huffington Post's six disruptors in business, alongside Steve Jobs and Mark Zuckerberg. In 2016, Goldin launched The Kara Network, a digital resource and mentoring platform for aspiring and established entrepreneurs. On her podcast, Unstoppable, she interviews founders, entrepreneurs, and disruptors across various industries.

. . . .

Both my parents passed away a few years ago, and each had a significant impact on me for different reasons. When I started kindergarten, my mom decided to go back to work after being home with the five of us kids for many years. My dad was super supportive but concerned because he didn't know how to cook.

Most people would have just figured out how to cook, but my dad thought that since he worked for a large food company, Conagra, he would try to develop healthy meals that he could throw in the oven or microwave. The only frozen dinners available at the time weren't that great, so as a result, he created another option, and Healthy Choice was born.

He spoke about fisherman off the coast of Georgia and how they gave up their mornings to supply shrimp for the dinners. It taught me that it's not just about having a great product, it's also about the people. He was ahead of his time when he talked about food sourcing and storytelling around what he believed people ultimately wanted. To this day, Healthy Choice is one of the top product lines at Conagra.

People ask me, "How did you decide to start a purpose-driven brand?" I didn't think of it in that way. I was always inquisitive and saw my father focusing on his "Why?" so I did the same with my company, Hint Inc. As someone who was addicted to diet soda and sweet-tasting drinks, I was determined to develop a healthy alternative.

I learned another lesson from my dad when I decided to move from Arizona to New York. I wanted to write for Fortune magazine but had no job offer. I was freaking out and thinking I shouldn't go, so I asked my father for advice. He had me estimate how much it would cost to get to JFK airport and fly back to Phoenix if necessary. Realizing it was not terribly expensive, he said, "You won't have any furniture and maybe you will have a lease for a year, but you do have a couple of credit cards. Although it wouldn't be great if you had to come home, you could do it." He helped me think about risk in that way.

Now I tell people, including my kids, that when you're on the fence, you have to think about the learning, not the failing. You don't have to build some big analysis. You can quickly write out the worst-case scenario, decide if you can afford it, and think about what you will gain from the experience. It's not just about the money; it's about the journey. Going to New York proved pivotal. Although I didn't get the editorial job I wanted, Fortune hired me on the circulation desk and it taught me a ton about what consumers wanted. I learned about working hard, showing up, rolling up your sleeves, and helping your neighbors even if they don't work in your group. People always remember the hard workers who were kind and funny.

My mom influenced me in a different way. She'd been an art history major at the University of Minnesota and loved art for a long time before deciding to enter the world of fashion. She had started a program in the Scottsdale, Arizona, public schools, to teach kids how to appreciate fine art, and at her funeral, people told me that was what they remembered most about her. But despite being comfortable with what she knew, she dared to reinvent herself. She wanted to do something different and showed me that it's about finding your passion and doing what you want to do even if some people tell you that you can't.

And then there is my husband, Theo—Hint's chief operating officer and my marvelous life partner. He was a fantastic intellectual property attorney before joining Hint. Initially, he came on board because he thought Hint was a completely crazy idea, and I was writing substantial personal checks from our bank account. I was okay living with one foot hanging off a cliff, but he was tentative. However, he believed 100 percent in me and my mission of getting people off sweet drinks and onto a healthier path, and once he heard me saying, "We can do this," he was all in. Law was getting a little boring, and he knew he could add massive value to Hint. He has brought the brand to the next level with innovative packaging and ideas.

Most important, he believes we should support each other. He knew my parents were there for each other no matter how crazy their ideas may have seemed to other people. Finding that kind of support is vital and something we talk about with our kids. Everyone needs to surround themselves with people who believe in their mission—be it friends, mates, or business partners. I can thank all of them for teaching me never to say, "I can't."

Instead, I say, "I'll try."

Brandon Gracey

Brandon Gracey is a technology executive and consultant to high-growth software companies and isn't quite sure what he wants to be when he grows up. He fills his time with travel, writing, red wine, triathlons, and arguing about politics. He lives in New York City with his wife, Lauren. He enjoys piña coladas and long walks on the beach.

. . . .

When I'd been selling software in one way or another for maybe ten years, my girlfriend (now wife) Lauren had been a nurse for about the same amount of time, and we'd been together for about half of that.

I was building the sales team for a startup and dealing with all the bull that comes with it: trouble making the right hires, not enough leads, deals that were supposed to close not closing, and a hierarchy of people who wanted answers on why and what we were going to do about it.

I came home from work one day, and Lauren, who had beat me home, asked me the same question asked to the second set of feet across the doorstep in almost every house in the world: "How was your day?"

Or maybe she didn't ask. It was one of those days when she was going to get an answer to that question whether she asked or not.

"It was a bear," I said before my shoes were off. "So-and-so changed their forecast, the CEO got pressure from the board and let me have it, a prospect won't return our rep's calls, and I got into an argument with a cab driver on the way home."

Lauren listened, nodded along, and offered sympathy for what was likely an entirely unsympathetic monologue. She asked questions about how I handled the problems and what I was going to do going forward. She completely put aside whatever she wanted to talk about and let me go till I was out of steam.

"Sorry, I've been talking since I walked in the door. How was your day?" I finally got around to asking her ten minutes after I started complaining.

My wife is a nurse, and it's in no way a stretch to say she cures cancer for a living. She's been an oncology nurse her whole career, and honestly she started before that because she helped nurse her father while he lost his battle with cancer when she was fifteen.

She asked: "Do you remember my patient? The woman who was a little older than me, with the two young kids? The one I really liked?"

"Of course, how is she?" I asked. I was still so focused on a missed sales number and an angry boss that I hadn't noticed that she didn't say, "The woman who IS a little older than me."

"She passed away today."

With that, the weight of my bullshit disappeared. Those four words delivered the most impactful perspective the professional side of me will ever receive.

We talked about her patient for much of the rest of the night. I tried to be as good a partner as Lauren had just been. I tried to listen, nod along, offer sympathy for what was an entirely sympathetic situation. I asked questions about how she handled it and how she talked with the patient's husband afterword. I learned for the first time how heavily a professional caretaker can carry the pain of the loss of their patients and how no one, by and large, cares about how they feel or how they're doing. I learned that a nurse's work problems are truly problems, but a nurse rarely sees them that way.

Ten minutes after getting home, which was ten minutes too late, I completely put aside what I wanted to talk about because I realized how significantly my problems weren't problems at all.

I'm not sure how good an employee or boss I am, but I believe that to the extent that I'm useful in tense situations and work "emergencies," it is because Lauren taught me on that night, and countless others since, about perspective. Nothing in my professional life has helped me more than understanding that no matter what I'm doing and no matter how big or impactful I believe the decisions I'm making are, at the end of the day, I'm not curing cancer.

Brett Hughes

Brett Hughes is a connector of people, projects, and purpose. He is a University of Virginia graduate, captain of UVA's NCAA championship team, and professional lacrosse captain and all-star. He is also the founder of the international nonprofit Lacrosse the Nations, where his passions for sport and service continue to collide. He builds companies through community, creativity, and teamwork and is a coach and mentor of young athletes through various stages of recruiting and life. He has a deep passion for travel, finding the most creative path to the top of the hill, connecting with others, and embracing the art of competition in everyday life.

. . . .

If you have ever landed a big deal, married the guy/girl of your dreams, or won a championship of some kind, maybe you have felt that moment— the moment right after the explosion of excitement when you are not sure what the emotion is, but you know you earned it and you know it is good. It's a mix of gratitude, joy, and exhaustion that comes from accomplishing something that is meaningful in ways that can't really be described no matter how many authors better than me have tried.

I am lucky to have experienced a good number of those, including championships, creating purpose-driven missions, and marrying the girl of my dreams. But most of us who have hit those milestones know all too well about the sweet and sour. You can't just camp out and live on Mount Everest. At some point, you have to come down or realize that the real mountain is higher still.

When I retired from competitive athletics, I "came down" so to speak and in some respects am still hunting for the next challenge in life because I will always be curious. I am lucky to have formed an amazing team with my nonprofit Lacrosse the Nations and a great team with my incredible wife, Kate Voegele. I am proud to have forged small communities with those I mentor and the people who mentor and advise me. Those feelings of winning championships and waking up the next day with the "what nexts" are sentiments that are very real to me.

Sometimes I think I know what's next, and other times, I am just not sure. At times, I have chosen to follow the path that my 10,000 hours have afforded me, and other times, I want to lend those 10,000 hours to fields and ideas and communities where I become the new kid on the block and go back to being student rather than teacher.

There are times in your life when you wake up and things are just clicking. You have a packed schedule, everything on that schedule is meaningful, and you are in fifth gear. Other times, you are hovering between neutral, first gear, and even reverse. I have come to realize that both seasons are incredibly important, useful, and flat-out necessary. Sometimes you need to decorate the room in your mind and soul and discover what's working and what isn't. The scary thing about doing that, of course, is that you are the architect, and only you can have the final say. But imagine if you could hire a creative guru to work alongside you and bring in pieces, ideas, and viewpoints that you never knew were possible.

Enter Ken Black—the man to whom I would like to give a standing ovation. I know firsthand that Ken is a living master class at unlocking the mind and allowing the individual to see the world with new eyes, pivot to a new idea or opportunity, or attack the same problem with a new set of tools.

Ken has encouraged me to realize that not only am I unique, but the uniqueness in everyone I collaborate with is the magic that makes partnerships and teams thrive. In a recent talk I had with him before he addressed a major college football program, we discussed how everyone should see themselves as unique, celebrate that, and then realize that their careers and life paths could be just as unique if they allow themselves to creatively design them.

What I love about Ken is that he is willing to share his knowledge with so many—from his Pivot Co-Lab program, which was one of the most amazing experiences I have had professionally, to his ability to unlock something in anyone through his talks, his work, and his leadership.

Among the many amazing accolades Ken has to his name is his creation of SPARQ, an athletic performance company that Nike bought. As a designer working for Nike, Ken also conceptualized and reinvented how basketball uniforms looked in the 1990s and created the Air Jordan XI with Tinker Hatfield. When he recently wrote me about his experience creating pieces that are still very much a part of what makes Nike a household name, Ken said something that resonates for me every day: "Instead of setting the expectation of making a bestselling basketball shoe, we decided to tell the most amazing story ever told."

If there's anything Ken knows better than anyone, it's the importance of great storytelling, and I'm always inspired by how he and his team did that for Michael Jordan, with the medium being a shoe.

Now Ken is following his own path tackling new problems and bringing his master class on the road. You will undoubtedly experience or see his work one way or another, and if you have ever bought or admired Nike products, chances are you already have in some way. There are few people who can start with design thinking, apply it to somebody's life and career path, and then listen patiently in the most humble position while they unlock themselves and their next steps.

To my friend, mentor, advisor, and catalyst Ken Black: Thank you for your guidance. I know that anyone who gets the chance to work with you, for you, or even near you will somehow come away with a couple new colors to paint their pictures with.

There is living and there is life and there is living a life. You continue to do the latter!

Cheers, my brother.

Morgan J. Ingram is director of execution and evolution at JBarrows Sales Training, where he focuses on helping sales development teams enhance their skill sets and performance. Previously, as sales development manager at Terminus, he managed a team of thirteen sales development representatives to help business-to-business marketers do account-based marketing at scale. He joined Terminus in early 2016 and helped the company become the fastest-growing startup in Atlanta. He has produced more than 100 videos that provide SDRs with motivation, advice, and tactics for his YouTube channel, The SDR Chronicles.

. . . .

My standing O goes to someone who helped accelerate my career, and his name is Carl King.

Carl and I met randomly on an airplane. After graduation, my parents told me to visit my uncle because he had started a company and been very successful in running it. The company I'd launched had failed, which led to me having no money in my bank account. So with an optimistic mindset, I headed to Dallas to see my uncle and get some advice on how to get back on my feet.

However, that advice came from a random stranger.

Carl sat down next to me on the flight and noticed that I was reading *The Law of Success*. He said, "Hey, great book you are reading there." I thanked him and said I appreciated it.

The next thing he said blew me away: "I have a message for you. You need to be doing public speaking, and you aren't living out your purpose at all right now."

Needless to say, that was a massive wake-up call. He had my full attention, and I asked him what I needed to do to become a public speaker. It was crazy because this had been on my mind for awhile.

During the flight, we wrote down a game plan of what I needed to do to become a public speaker. After that conversation, he gave me the spirit to attack my dream with full force. Five years later, I am living out the dream that we wrote down together.

So here's my shout-out to Carl for sitting next to me on the plane that day. And I am thankful that we have continued to stay connected since that encounter.

Mike Katz

Former NFL player and professional bodybuilder Mike Katz is probably best known for his appearance in Pumping Iron *in 1977 with Arnold Schwarzenegger. His achievements in the world of bodybuilding include a record of titles and accomplishments too numerous to list. At age seventy-four, he still trains several times a week and enjoys judging the occasional bodybuilding contest. He continues to be an inspiration to athletes everywhere and is a testament to what a lifetime of treating a body well can produce in terms of health, stamina, and resilience, both physically and emotionally.*

. . . .

I grew up in a middle-class neighborhood of a nice town with two loving parents who were excellent role models for me. However, I needed a lot of direction, and it was my seventh-grade health education teacher, Mr. Gerosa, who influenced me the most.

I was in a little punk gang, and I met him at a time when I could have gone in one of two directions. I decided very early in life that I wanted to be like him, helping kids and giving them the right information so that they could make the best decisions possible. Luckily, with his influence on me, I was able to maneuver my life down the right path, and for thirty-five years, I was a health education teacher. I loved every day that I taught and the impact I was able to have on my students.

Mr. Gerosa was a Marine with spit-shined shoes and a shiny bald head that rivaled them. We would always fool around with him, pretending to polish the top of his head. He was an influential, no-nonsense guy, but he was also a very fair and warm-hearted fellow. As a teacher, he made the class informative, useful to me, and helpful in the crucial decisions that young kids often have to make.

Some of the things he taught me were compassion for other people, sensitivity, and respect toward life and the challenges we face. He was able to connect real-life situations to decisions that kids, as well as adults, would have to make and put us in positions where we had an opportunity to brainstorm ways in which we could become better people. We learned to stop bullying if we were picking on other kids, make better choices about smoking and alcohol, and respect our girlfriends and other women. When we got out of line, he knew how to get us back in, and when we did things to his liking academically, he knew how to reward us in a very fair way.

I've accomplished quite a bit in life. I played with the Jets and Joe Namath, traveled the world with Arnold Schwarzenegger, and was in two movies. I was the co-star of *Pumping Iron* and featured in a documentary. Arnold was a big part of my bodybuilding success, along with Harold Helland, but I still point to Mr. Gerosa as deserving of my standing O. If I didn't have him as a leader and role model during those years of my life, maybe I would have taken the wrong road.

I certainly took the right one, and I give him a lot of credit for teaching me how to be a man as opposed to the boy that I was. He got me through adolescence, which are difficult years for boys, and I thank him every chance I get.

Kathy Leckey is vice president of SomethingNew, helping Scott MacGregor, Jaime Lannon Diglio, and the team disrupt the talent optimization space. She is a former TEDx speaker, mentor, and event organizer. Her behind-the-TEDx-scenes interview was featured on the Be the Talk *podcast. She is the active mother of three teenagers and their dog, Buddy, and is happiest when with her family and friends, especially at the beach. She is very active in the community and volunteers with local organizations, including the Look for the Good Project. She believes gratitude is the most simple and effective way to find true happiness.*

. . . .

When I sat down to be interviewed by members of the TEDx committee, I expected to tell them about how my son, who was eight years old at the time, had learned that almost 6,000 children die each day from water-related diseases so he started a campaign to raise awareness and money to send LifeStraw filters to provide clean drinking water to communities in Africa. I told them how his speaking engagements throughout the state prompted his older and younger sisters to found their own organizations. With the nonprofit I started, our family had been bringing friends and school groups together to allow more young kids to experience the impact giving back can have on your life no matter how old you are.

As expected, the committee members were impressed by what I told them and wanted to hear more. However, the conversation shifted when I told them our family had been completely upended when my husband was sentenced to three years in prison for charges related to his business. We had lost everything and moved from our small-town community in Connecticut to live in the city of Buffalo, New York, where we could be near family. What I didn't expect was for one of the women to lean across the table, put her hand on mine, and say, "You have something much bigger to say here."

Thirty days later, I was on the TEDx stage sharing the pain, challenges, and perceptions that were shaping our new reality. My standing O is to a woman who was a complete stranger, a woman who gave me the courage to speak my truth. The whole truth. I had come to talk about all the amazing things my kids were doing, not the trauma we were experiencing, but in the end I chose to share it all in front of the audience that day, including my children.

I shared the three most important choices I have learned to make when faced with circumstances beyond my control. The first choice is the perspective I take on the situation and on how important the issue really is. Is it life or death? Could it be worse? Will it matter a year from now? Most often, it is not as bad as the initial thoughts, fears, and worries surrounding it are.

The second choice is looking at difficult circumstances as opportunities to learn. What can this situation teach me about myself and where I need to grow? We learned grit and resilience over time. We learned to live without some of the material things we had been used to having, and we learned the difference between wanting and needing. We learned the appreciation of the small things. All of a sudden, things we had taken for granted became a treat. We learned the importance of family and friends who supported us in so many ways and always gave us a safe place to come home. We learned to live in a very different community from our small town in Connecticut. Life in the city taught us all kinds of lessons and made us stronger. When we moved back to Connecticut, my children came back with an entirely different appreciation for the schools, their teachers, and the community that welcomed them back.

The third choice is deciding whether to be the victim or be empowered. At first, I found myself playing the part of the victim. I noticed one night at a school function where I was normally very outgoing and involved that I had dressed down, wore no makeup, and was standing back in the shadows as if somehow I had changed and didn't deserve to be there anymore. I worried that my kids would become victims of the situation and become depressed, addicted, or worse—until I realized that they could use what they learned about themselves through adversity to become artists, writers, or athletes. I knew had to be an example for them by choosing gratitude, love, and truth and by choosing to engage completely rather than hide behind embarrassment or shame.

Those three choices shaped my thoughts about the past, present, and future. The importance of this is found in Gandhi's words: "Your beliefs become your thoughts. Your thoughts become your words. Your words become your actions. Your actions become your habits. Your habits become your values. Your values become your destiny."

I was right when I said we had a long way to go. Since I was on that stage, I have had to continue to make those choices every day as I deal with the challenges that many people deal with, including divorce, being a single parent, moving to another state, career, health, and everything else life brings. I have to constantly choose to see them as opportunities to learn and grow and recognize that the important thing is the choices we make, not the situations in which we find ourselves.

Being a TEDx speaker has opened opportunities for me and fast-tracked new and more meaningful friendships and relationships. People feel like they can be honest with me without being judged and with no pressure to keep up with me. It set the tone for the way we handled that situation and the way we handle new opportunities to learn each day. For that, I am forever grateful to Stacey Watson-Mesley for getting me up on that stage and encouraging me to speak the truth.

Shari Levitin

Shari Levitin is an energetic, wickedly funny sales guru who helps teams bridge the gap between beating quota and selling with an authentic, heartfelt approach. As founder of the Shari Levitin Group, she has helped create more than $1 billion in increased revenue for companies in more than forty countries. She is the bestselling author of Heart and Sell: 10 Universal Truths Every Salesperson Needs to Know *and is a contributor to* Forbes, CEO Magazine, Quotable, Inc. magazine *and* Huffington Post.

. . . .

I have a confession to make. I started my career as a less-than-mediocre salesperson. I spent five years selling very little and making even less. And then I had one extraordinary week.

I was working late when my manager, Greg (not his real name), approached me and said, "Shari, I need to see you before you leave tonight."

I finished writing up the client contract I was working on and started the long walk to his office. My mouth was dry. I found myself subconsciously trying to control my strangely ragged breaths. I couldn't imagine what I'd done. I'd never been called into the boss's office before. I had to keep my lips from quivering, and I avoided making eye contact with him.

He sat me down, closed the office door, looked me in the eye, and said, "I've been in this business for eighteen years. I've been watching you. You have a rare talent. If you keep learning and training, you have the ability to be number one in the industry."

I couldn't believe it. Not only was I not in trouble, I was getting praise I'd never gotten before. "If you keep up the good work and invest in a little more training, you have the ability to be one of the best salespeople this industry has ever seen," he added.

I left his office with my head held high, feeling reenergized and excited. The next morning, I arrived extra early—clearly, I had all this talent I needed to nurture. I read every book on sales strategy, psychology, and decision-making I could find.

At the end of that year, I was the number one salesperson at our sales site. In the second year, I was the number one salesperson in our entire company.

I'd worked harder than I ever had in my life, and along the way, with each accomplishment, Greg congratulated me on my "rare talent." Eventually, he made me a manager.

Two months later, I found that my "rare talent" didn't extend to managing. I was a miserable failure at my new post. Half my team liked me, the other half hated me, and those sides would flip flop back and forth every day. I couldn't do anything right. I finally walked into Greg's office and said, "I'm not cut out for management."

"What took you so long?" was his reply.

"When you were a salesperson," he continued, "you came in asking for training and help almost daily. Now that you're a manager, you seem to think you should already know it all."

My eyes welled up with tears.

"Are you going to quit?" he asked, and I shook my head through my tears. "Or do you want me to teach you how to be the world's greatest sales manager?"

I nodded.

"Okay, listen," he said, "You're going to have many salespeople work for you throughout your career. Some will be good, some won't. But when you find one who's willing to learn, even if they're not that good, sit them down, close your office door, look them in the eye, and tell them that they have a rare talent. Tell them that with a little bit of training, they have the ability to become number one in the industry."

I was furious. "Are you telling me all this time you've been saying that I have a rare talent, you didn't mean it?"

Greg laughed so hard he just about fell off his chair. "What difference does it make?"

Suddenly, I got it. It didn't matter if I'd had a "rare talent" in the beginning or not. It didn't matter if Greg was just making it up. What mattered was that he had the rare ability to find the talent in others, and in doing so, he helped me believe in myself.

He taught me a life lesson I now refer to as forced optimism. Every day, in every encounter, you have a choice. You can look for what's right in a person or situation, or you can look for what's wrong or missing. Throughout my life, whenever I focus on what's working rather than what's lacking, my confidence and my success grow exponentially.

Chaunté Lowe

Chaunté Lowe is a motivational speaker and a professional athlete who is an American record holder, a four-time Olympian, a three-time World Championship medalist, and a twelve-time U.S. National Champion. She realized her childhood dream of competing in the Olympics when she was twenty years old and was the first woman from Georgia Tech's track and field team to become an Olympian. The following year, she won silver at the 2005 World Championships and became the first American woman to win a world outdoor championship medal in the high jump since 1983. She will be training for her fifth Olympics while battling breast cancer.

. . . .

I have had the amazing opportunity to compete in track and field for Team USA as a world-class athlete for fifteen years. Much like tennis, track and field is an individual sport where every man is out for himself. In training, the focus is on self-motivation, self-determination, and self-execution. Whether or not you win your race is solely a product of how you perform in comparison to your competitors. Did you jump higher? Did you run faster? Did you throw farther?

That type of environment is a breeding ground for narcissism, individualism, and self-pride. In my case, however, with every accolade received, I knew I could never forget the contributions of those who helped me get there. This was especially true when I won the bronze medal at the 2008 Summer Olympic Games in Beijing.

I came from very humble beginnings. I remember sitting at the park as a child and watching other children practice sports as I fought back tears. I wanted to play so badly, but my family couldn't afford the fees associated with participation. When I finally got the opportunity to participate in sports in the public school system, I gave it everything I had. I was finally able to be part of something that I had only experienced from the sidelines.

When I was in high school, finances were still a struggle, but coaches, family members, and friends chipped in to replace my tattered shoes, give me rides to practices, and pay for travel to national championships. Those contributions led to me earning a full athletic scholarship and meeting the man who made the single largest contribution to one of the most fulfilling moments of my life.

My college coach, Nat Page, was a phenomenal athlete who had competed professionally in both the high jump and the 400-meter hurdles. He had a dream of competing in the Olympics, and that dream had almost come true in 1980 when he qualified to represent America in the high jump at the Summer Olympic Games in Moscow. Unfortunately, politics interrupted his date with destiny because the U.S. boycotted the competition in response to the Soviet Union's invasion of Afghanistan in 1979. Rather than regretting the opportunity he'd lost, Nat turned his attention to developing other athletes through coaching. I was blessed enough to be one of those athletes.

He coached me to my first Olympic team in 2004, but it wasn't until 2008 that I realized how much I needed him. In the summer of 2007, my husband and I had our first child, I was trying to finish my college degree, and I still had to prepare for the 2008 Olympic Games. I was scared because our livelihood depended on me making that team. Every single day, Nat met me at our training site and coached me.

My fitness was catastrophically depleted, and we didn't have much to work with at first. The prospect of making the team seemed hopeless. Bit by bit, he would increase the intensity of my training to a point where I was not comfortable but wouldn't leave the practice feeling defeated. Each day I would get stronger and closer to wearing Team USA's red, white, and blue again. Some days I wanted to stop, but he wouldn't let me quit. When I felt as though the task was impossible, he was there to build a case for my success. He convinced me that even though it was hard, it was not impossible and showed me that I didn't have to make this journey alone because he would be with me every step of the way.

When the time came, I won the Olympic trials and made it onto my second Olympic team. I ended up placing sixth in China with pride because of the journey it took to get there. Never once did Nat encourage me to cheat, use performance-enhancing drugs, or take any other shortcuts. We tackled this beast the long, hard, and right way.

That level of integrity came with a bonus. In 2016, eight years after the games, it was discovered that several of the top finishers had cheated, and they were disqualified. Subsequently, the results were invalidated, and my placement was upgraded to the bronze medal. I was awarded the medal at an amazing ceremony with Nat in attendance. If it weren't for his dedication and mentorship, I would not be an Olympic medalist. I owe him my gratitude and so much more. Thank you, Nat, for your contributions to my life.

Over the years, he taught me many valuable lessons that have become ingrained into the fabric of who I am, including:

1. Never take a shortcut now that will cost you in the future. Those words kept me from skipping practices, allowing lazy or sloppy technique, and most importantly, cheating to gain an edge over competitors.

2. Never do anything in the dark that you don't want to see come to light. A good reputation takes a lifetime to develop, but with a misstep, it can be lost in an instant.

3. Take ownership of everything that is within your control. You can't control the weather, political unrest, someone else's performance, or many of the obstacles that come your way. But you can prepare for as many different situations as possible and make sure that you are ready to rise to the occasion when obstacles present themselves.

Joe Maloy

Joe Maloy is an Olympian and World Champion triathlete who, in addition to competing at endurance events around the world, owns an online coaching practice and works with USA Triathlon to recruit collegiate athletes into the triathlon. Throughout his career, he has represented the U.S. in twenty-two countries on six continents. Some of his professional highlights include anchoring Team USA to its first world championship in the mixed-team relay and crossing the line as the top American male finisher at the 2016 Summer Olympics in Rio de Janeiro. He has also won the Escape from Alcatraz Triathlon and the Noosa Triathlon.

. . . .

When I was training to represent the U.S. in the triathlon at the 2016 Summer Olympics in Rio de Janeiro, my mind convinced my body that working out three times a day and thirty hours a week was normal. The elite athlete learns to normalize exceptional daily achievements in order to perform at a sport's highest levels. Perhaps relationships work the same way. Exceptional investment on a consistent basis can yield uncommon results. My parents, Joe and Mary Maloy, deserve a standing O for the way they modeled love and care while creating space for my brother, John, and me to grow.

One can never truly appreciate that which is closest until he or she achieves some type of distance. It's the nature of perspective. One's reality can only be described as "normal" until there's a different frame of reference.

John and I grew up in the small town of Wildwood Crest, on New Jersey's southern peninsula. My parents met when they both worked one summer on the Wildwood Crest Beach Patrol, and the chain of events thereafter had them raising a family in that same town. The only home I can remember is a three-bedroom, two-and-a-half-bath Cape Cod-style beach house that's a two-minute barefoot run from the beach.

Many American children grow up wanting things. Over the years, I remember wanting things, too—a Teddy Ruxpin toy, a pet dog, and a rat tail-style haircut, to name a few. My parents provided some of those things. They said no to the rat tail, though. Although I could write another standing O for the decision on that haircut, this note is to thank them for saying yes to spending time with my brother and me.

Like most American families, my parents each worked a full-time job and had individual interests, but they decided our time at the dinner table was sacred. We'd plan our meals for the week every Sunday, and they would be based around the many extracurricular commitments in which John and I were involved. My dad would do the grocery shopping, my mom would do the cooking, and I don't recall who did the dishes. I usually tried to be away from the kitchen and walking the dog for that part. (Despite my mom's apprehension, we did get the dog.)

My parents honored this time every night except for Thursdays. My mom played tennis on those nights, and my dad let us order take-out and eat atop a beach towel that we laid in front of the TV. It's the closest this Jersey kid ever got to having a picnic. Hey, six out of seven ain't bad.

My parents prioritized dinnertime as a space for us to enjoy nourishment. The meal brought us together, and the company kept us together. John and I knew it was okay to invite friends, and many times we had guests we didn't even know would be coming. Most of the town knew about our dinners, and whenever people couldn't get in touch with us, they knew we were most likely sitting and talking. "Come on in. Are you hungry?" my parents would ask. They made space and made the food work—it's the type of people they are. We shared food, drink, and perspective and learned to love one another while sitting around that table.

I'm grateful for the opportunity to give a standing O to my parents for normalizing something as exceptional as our family dinners. Reflecting on those times in our kitchen, I realize I never really wanted for anything as a kid because I had love and attention every night from the two people I most wanted to emulate. It's a tradition I'll be proud to share with a family of my own someday.

Of course, you're all invited. Just don't come empty-handed!

Scott Manthorne

Scott Manthorne is an entrepreneur, a single dad, a life strategist, and a philanthropist. He is a builder of networking communities for both business and charitable initiatives. He is also an expert in tactical business networking and the founder/partner of several successful companies that connect the athlete entrepreneur to business executives globally.

. . . .

In 1985, I was going to college in Florida and thinking I knew it all. Between all my studying, I often found my way to the local college bar and soon became close friends with the Proprietor.

Larry Kebberly was a stocky man, maybe fifteen years older than me. Jovial. Strong. Confident. He was built like a refrigerator. And as far as I was concerned, he was living the dream. Soon I found out about his achievements as an arm wrestling champ (no surprise) and a martial arts instructor (BIG surprise) who could stand belly to belly with you and still hit the back of your head with the inside of his foot (yes, it happened to me).

Far from being an athlete, I had zero interest in getting involved in martial arts. On top of that, I had no confidence that anything would come from it. My physical stats in high school were less than staggering (5'5", 135 pounds). No true relationship with a coach. What little did I know!

For almost three years, Master Kebberly hammered me, shamed me, and finally convinced me to try a contact sport. It changed my life forever. During my ten-year journey through martial arts, I learned several life-changing lessons. Each has had a profound impact on me.

- **Courtesy**. My fondest memory revolves around the dojo. Leaving your shoes outside is based on the philosophy that you left your problems at the door. And the emphasis was placed on treating every student the same regardless of rank, age, or gender. Courtesy is sometimes a lost gesture in our world.

- **Integrity**. I often participated in competitions, sometimes refereed, or attended as a spectator. In my day, many of the judges were Korean, and all instructions were given that way. I loved the way of the competition and the true integrity shown to all in the room. It was refreshing. It's how I strive to manage all my social interactions. It was a great gift to be part of this.

- **Perseverance**. In martial arts, ranks are earned and become more revered as the color gets darker (i.e., from white to black). I learned the hard way how tough it was to achieve my black belt, but I made it through. It was a true lesson in how a significant goal can be achieved, how a timeline often cannot be compressed, and how much effort goes into something that few ever achieve.

- **Indomitable spirit**. Some call it patience, persistence, or being stubborn. No matter how it's described, it's a character trait that shows itself eventually. Each day, I was pushed to my limits both mentally and physically. From this, I learned that we can always work harder, endure through tough times, and never give up. It has saved me often in business and helped with some tough personal challenges as well.

- **Self-control**. It has served me well over the years when sizing up business opportunities, responding to the solicited and unsolicited remarks of others, or taking a step back to evaluate what has been presented. It has been the foundation of my patience with others.

Other valuable lessons include:

1. Size up your opponent, and dare him to underestimate you.

2. Know your surroundings—who's in the room, who's in your market.

3. Be patient. All good things come in time.

4. Learn the basics to master the impossible.

My years in martial arts led me to being a coach, a business owner, a highly confident being, a humble servant, a grounded being, a proud man. I can't thank Master Kebberly enough.

Sadly, he passed away a few years ago. During the last years of his life, we had grown apart. When I heard of his illness, I reconnected—and just in time. Master Kebberly was near death, and it broke my heart. I thanked him from the bottom of my heart. I shared my standing O.

Businesses that want to increase revenue and profits and differentiate themselves in a competitive market ask for Bernadette McClelland. She has coached Harvard MBA students on sales enablement, been the Master Asia Pacific coach for Tony Robbins in twelve countries, written five books on leadership and sales transformation, and won a coveted (Australian) Telstra award for business excellence. She shares her ideas about personal responsibility, resilience, and resourcefulness on stages throughout the world. Reaching the pinnacle of corporate sales success at three Fortune 500 companies after having experienced the depths of bankruptcy positions her as a transparent, gutsy, and compelling speaker, coach, and writer.

. . . .

When we think about gratitude, there is someone we can thank every single day if we choose. Each person we come in contact with helps us in some way.

Everything we experience also has some kind of meaning, and being grateful for both those experiences and the people behind those experiences is important—regardless of whether those experiences are positive or negative.

From the local barista feeding our souls with coffee, the postal worker who delivers our parcels and window-faced envelopes, and yes, even the telemarketer who brings screen-time attention back into the real world at dinner time, there is always a place to give a "hat tip" and say thanks if we look.

It raises the question, though: How often do we stop and actually speak those words? Or more than saying thank you, how often do we attempt to appreciate what the people around us do and why?

So this request to contribute to *Standing O! Encore* and share gratitude for someone has caused me to think deeply.

Of course, the usual suspects who mean the world to me come to mind: my uber-supportive husband, Tim, and my children, Danni and Matt. And there is always Mum and Dad for bringing me into this world and my dear friends and colleagues with whom I share my life. Although they're not the immediate focus of this piece, their value will never diminish in my eyes. I will be forever grateful and always encourage them to take their own standing Os.

There have been many others without whose guidance I wouldn't be who I am nor where I am today. Being in Tony Robbins' world as one of his coaches immediately after going bankrupt epitomized what becoming a change-maker means. Being mentored by Matt Church of Thought Leaders was game-changing and helped launch my speaking business. My first coach, Cynthia Freeman, created an environment that was life-changing for me by holding me accountable to a much higher standard and broadening my world.

When I think about who has led me to where I am today, I also ponder people I would not normally consider because there is a time to thank those who have perhaps unwittingly helped.

Those who said, "You can't do it." Those who bullied and mocked. Those who have perhaps not shown as much love toward you as you needed. Those who excluded you from events or conversations. Those who said, "Who do you think you are?"

If you are anything like me, you wouldn't be where you are today without those people in your life. In my case, rather than blaming those people, I now thank them.

My school teacher Mrs. Gully, who sat me on my own in the middle of the oval, taught me resilience. My principal Sister Alphonsus, who constantly had it in for me, taught me tenacity. My parents, who said I'd be back from overseas in a week and not last eight months in another country, taught me independence. My boss who said I didn't have what it took to be in sales taught me the long game. My colleague who constantly bullied me taught me empathy. My siblings who don't practice forgiveness taught me to love regardless. My first online troll taught me faith in my abilities.

They all deserve to be front and center for just a minute—enough time for me to put my hands together, ask them to take a bow, and with a resounding standing O, realize it was always all about them.

People bring out in us what we need for each step of our lives, and I have become richer because these wonderful people have been in my life, not in spite of them having been in my life.

And for that I am grateful.

Linda McGuigan

Linda McGuigan is constantly aspiring to be a better servant leader. She believes success is achieved by inspiring and mentoring others. As an accomplished senior executive, entrepreneur, consultant to CEOs, and board member, she is known for her ability to connect people to one another and then foster the connection to strategic gain. She believes the key to achieving the desired organizational result is to develop teams that embody trust, respect, commitment, accountability, excellence, and a servant leader mindset. She has a passion for spreading this message in all aspects of her life, including to cherished friends and family, and believes there is nothing more rewarding than positioning people for success.

. . . .

When Scott MacGregor told me he was going to gift me the honor of contributing to *Standing O! Encore*, my first reaction was one of overwhelming gratitude. It was immediately followed by the choice to honor my beautiful niece Cara.

No one really knows what it is like to battle a life-threatening illness until that person is you. If you have ever had surgery, there is a moment just before you get the anesthesia—can you bring up the feeling you had? Perhaps the most alone you have ever felt, right? It is you and your thoughts, and if you believe in a higher self, you might have Him in your head. I would imagine that is what it feels like to hear that you have life-threatening cancer. You have to process that in your head, all by yourself. You walk around every waking moment of every day owning that realization and living that reality.

Cara with the gorgeous red hair and cackle laugh was seven years old when her mother, Sallie, died of breast cancer. Sallie was beautiful—Ivory Soap-model beautiful—and taken way too young at only thirty years old. Hers was the first adult death I had to deal with, and I was thirty at the time as well. Cara is like a daughter to me, and we share a bond. She loves me and loves the way I live. There is nothing like the feeling of family loving you for you; they certainly don't have to. Cara was eager to give, in spite of losing her mom at a young age, and she was anxious to have a family of her own. I live to give and serve, and to this day, Cara is a joyful, adorable, and fun mentee.

I will never forget where I was when I received that call, the one I had always dreaded. It was a Friday night in February 2017 and I was shopping at Fresh Markets in Duluth, Georgia. "Aunt Linda, I have a lump they are concerned about it." The world stopped.

On March 17, 2017, we learned that Cara had the BRCA1 gene. Our worst fears became reality, and within two months, she endured a radical mastectomy and reconstruction followed by twenty-four grueling months of chemo/Herceptin and a radical hysterectomy on June 5, 2018. Thirteen months later, Cara was clean. She persevered with the help of her faith, grit, determination, vulnerability, humor, and ALL the love surrounding her from family and friends.

For me, inspiration happens when I see courage overcome fear, authenticity in the battle, and the determination to continue on. Cara could easily be gripped by the circumstances, but she is not. She is teaching me how to be the best aunt I can be by being the best Cara she can be.

She is thriving, one day at a time, along with her amazing husband, Chris, and three beautiful children—Zak, Sophie, and Clark. Cara is my joy and inspiration.

David Meltzer

David Meltzer is CEO and co-founder of Sports 1 Marketing, one of the world's most renowned sports marketing firms. He has been recognized as sports humanitarian of the year by Variety *and serves as chairman of the board for the Unstoppable Foundation, which brings sustainable education to children and communities in developing countries, thereby creating a safer and more just world for everyone. He is a two-time international bestselling author and top 100 business coach who has spent twenty-five years working as an entrepreneur and executive in the legal, technology, sports, and entertainment fields.*

. . . .

It's not often that a birthday party changes your life. And it's even less common to have someone else's birthday change your life, but that's what happened to me.

Birthday parties can be self-indulgent and extravagant. Or when done correctly, they can change the world in a single evening.

My good friend and mentor Cynthia Kersey not only changed my life with a birthday, she changed the world.

While attending a women's conference in rural Africa, she learned about some of the struggles of the local women and was inspired to make a difference in their lives. She didn't know that she would also make a profound difference in my life.

Cynthia chose to dedicate her fiftieth birthday to a fundraising event for some of the women she had met on her journey and, as a result, ended up raising enough money to build two schools in Uganda. She changed thousands of lives in a single evening. That birthday experience led her to create the Unstoppable Foundation, which helps bring sustainable education to children and communities in developing countries, changing their lives as well as the lives of future generations.

Cynthia's dedication to serving others with vision and purpose has become a beacon to me. Her commitment to ensuring that every child gets access to education and her desire to eradicate poverty around the world resonated with me, which is why I began working with Unstoppable.

In fact, I was so inspired by Cynthia's birthday story that I dedicated my fiftieth birthday to fundraising for Unstoppable. Actually, my plan as chairman of the foundation's board was to throw fifty fundraising parties at places around the world in order to follow Cynthia's lead and build a leadership and empowerment center in Kenya. The "50 for 50" campaign was so successful that we ended up building two community centers in Kenya.

That brings me to the lesson I learned through this experience and the reason I will forever be grateful to Cynthia for empowering me to empower others to be happy. Nothing beats unconditionally giving to others. When you give, it releases "feel good" chemicals in the brain of the person who is receiving. It also releases those same chemicals in your brain when you give. But the real beauty of giving is that people who witness giving experience the exact same reaction.

Giving unconditionally, being abundant, and living to be of service to others has changed my life for the better. And for that, I give my great friend Cynthia Kersey a standing ovation.

Mark Metry

Mark Metry is the host of the Humans 2.0 *podcast, which has been featured in* Forbes *and* Yahoo! Finance *and was included on a list of the "Top 21 Growing Podcasts You Must Listen to in 2019." His show features the greatest leaders of our time, and he frequently converses with billionaires, professional athletes, Pulitzer Prize-winning journalists, and* New York Times *bestselling authors exploring the dynamic of the human experience in modern technological times. He delivers transformative talks, workshops, and keynotes about human potential, mindset, mental health, and social anxiety as well as using podcasting as a business.*

· ·

Today I am a happy twenty-two-year-old living the best possible life I could be living here on planet Earth. I am successful in every sense even though I came from material lack and struggled with my mental health. Nobody can give you happiness other than yourself. I am self-made in this respect, but I have encountered so many kind, loving souls during my journey who have helped me, supported me, and taught me invaluable lessons that no doubt created the person I am today—the one who speaks around the world and on my top 100 podcast *Humans 2.0*.

I am proud to say I am a first-generation American from Egyptian immigrant parents. My parents seized the opportunity to move to America a couple years before I was born in 1997. With only $200 in their pockets and a heart full of courage and love, they set out to expand the Metry empire into new territories with the hope of giving their kids better opportunities.

I am just beginning to understand what my parents went through to give me the opportunity to be successful. I'm not just talking about leaving their country and everything they knew for hope but for the amazing lessons they taught me along the way.

My father, Rezk Metry, taught me lessons about integrity that set the foundation for how I operate on a daily basis. When I was young, he would tell me inspirational quotes about working hard and constantly trying and growing no matter what you do. As a kid, I didn't understand exactly what he was talking about, but looking back now, those elements became the foundation of my psychology.

One particularly impactful lesson took place at a pet store when I was thirteen years old. I loved going to the pet store and exploring all the different kinds of fish. One day, I bought three fish that each cost $2.99. As we were driving home, I realized that the woman at the cash register had only charged me $2.99 for all three fish. My dad turned the car around and said we had to return to the store and give her the remaining $6.

I didn't understand why my father would take the time to go all the way back, and it irritated me. When we explained to the woman, she apologized for her mistake and told us to keep the fish without paying the full price. Looking back at this event, I realize that it changed the course of my life because I learned the importance of being honest no matter what. If you are honest with the world, the world will treat you fairly.

My father was not the only person who influenced me toward greatness. My loving sister Maggi is why I matured into the person I am today. She and I grew up in an immigrant culture in which you have only a few career choices: doctor, lawyer, engineer, or failure.

So what did my sister do? She said screw it. She wanted to become an English teacher in the public schools because that's what she loves to do, and she wanted to teach kids a practical skill the same way she had to learn English when she came to America. Maggi set the precedent in our household and community that you can do what you want while helping people, and it doesn't matter what other people say or think about you.

My sweetheart mother, Hannan, has taught me so many lessons that I could write an entire book about them. Aside from encouraging me to get involved in community and social initiatives, my mom taught me the importance of valuing my future more than what's going on right now. When something happened or maybe we got into a fight, she would say,

"It's a new page" or "Let's start a new page" in the ultimate book of life. Applying my mother's concept has been invaluable in carving my own future-oriented path in life and has given me the exponential skill of constantly moving no matter what obstacles I am faced with.

Kristi Neilan is the owner of Body Fusion by Excel, a wife, and a stepmother of two. She is a certified personal trainer and Spartan SGX coach. She is a former World Natural Bodybuilding Federation pro figure competitor and in 2018 finished second in her age group in the Spartan U.S. National Series. She has also completed Hell on the Hill and 29029 Everesting. She continues to be a competitive obstacle course racing athlete and has completed her first ultramarathon. She enjoys helping people reach their physical potential and spends her free time racing and fundraising for the Semper Fi Fund.

. . . .

I have come from a long line of strong women. Some of them were teenage moms, wives of alcoholics, and in some unfortunate circumstances, victims of abusive men. Each generation had their struggles and always wanted better despite the cards they were dealt. It was a lifestyle we knew as normal.

When I turned fifteen, my mother asked me to break that cycle. It was inevitable where my life was going. My grades had been slipping since I was nine, and I was always in trouble for fighting—not just at school but at home. So I agreed. I made a promise to my mom to break the cycle.

After I had just barely graduated high school, she came to me again. This time she wasn't asking, she was telling. "Kris, it's time for you to move out." I had no college future. All I knew was how to work and how to survive emotionally, but still I doubted myself. "Mom, what if I can't make it? What if I can't pay my rent?" She looked at me with the saddest eyes and said, "I've raised you to be strong. You will figure it out. But you can't keep living here. All you do it fight with your father."

That was true. I was angry all the time, and his drinking didn't make matters any better. It was how he coped with his own trauma and his own demons—the family curse. So I took every emotion I had and channeled it. I figured it out. Failure was not an option, neither was going back home. My future was solely on me. I worked three jobs and paid my rent, car insurance, gas, and food all at the age of eighteen. Once I realized I could do it, I wanted more. I wanted an education.

I tried enlisting in the military but failed the Armed Services Vocational Aptitude Battery test three times. I had attention deficit disorder. I had managed to pass grade school and high school without ever reading a book. But that lack of effort found its way into my immediate future. I had no one to copy off and no teacher to persuade in order to get that passing grade. I knew I had to find something else, something more hands-on if I wanted a better life for myself. My future had to be something I could do physically.

That's when I came across the National Personal Training Institute, which offered both hands-on and classroom learning. That was my ticket out. So I found a way to take out a loan in my name and enrolled immediately. My grandparents let me live with them for a few months so I could save enough money to move to Florida and get an education. For the first time in my life, I had found something I was good at, something I could focus on. The human body amazed me. I had no idea how physically capable we are as humans. And when you combine that with a strong mental toughness, you will achieve things you never thought possible.

After graduating from the institute, I started taking on more physical challenges. I pushed my body past perceived limitations. I learned that I could win my figure pro card in under a year of competing, run a sub-four-hour marathon, run an ultramarathon, and not only podium a Spartan Race but place second in my age group and twenty-first overall in a national series.

So my standing O doesn't just go to fitness, it goes to something greater. My standing O goes to STRONG WOMEN. To my mother, her mother, and her mother's mother. It goes to my sister and every woman out there who had to take nothing and turn it into something. It is up to us to pass the torch to the next generation of women and teach them that no matter what obstacles life gives you, you can be unstoppable.

Mark Neilan

Mark Neilan is the owner of Excel Fitness Center, a husband, and father of two. He has a bachelor's degree in biology from the College of New Jersey, a master's of physical therapy from the University of Saint Augustine, and a doctoral degree in physical therapy from Temple University. He has competed in eighteen marathons (personal record of 2:50:09) and finished Jesse Itzler's Hell on the Hill race three times. In 2018, Neilan was the first to complete 29029 Everesting and finished second overall in the Spartan Age Group National Series. In the past six years, he has raised more than $400,000 for the Semper Fi Fund.

. . . .

The underdog mentality gets my standing O. There are positives and negatives to that mentality, but I believe that is why I am where I am today.

The underdog mentality has been my specialty. I was never the strongest, fastest, or most agile, but I wanted to be. As a young boy, I could not climb the rope or do a pull-up or push-up, and I finished almost last in the forty-yard dash. I hated not being able to do what the other boys my age were doing. When I started playing baseball, I thought I had found my true passion, something I could compete in—until I found myself walking down the first baseline with my coach. He said, "You won't be starting in the next game. There are some kids who have it and some who don't. You're not that kid, Mark, so you better start thinking about coaching when you get older, not playing."

My thirteen-year-old mind did not know how to process that. I was hurt and humiliated. The one sport I thought I was good at and my coach just took it away in a matter of seconds. That's when it happened, that feeling when a fire is lit in your belly. It starts way down deep inside and builds. It talks to you and then fuels you. You become focused with only your mission in mind. I may not have made it to the major leagues, but I continued playing throughout high school and during my freshman year of college despite what that coach saw in me.

During college and graduate school, that fire stayed lit. I played in lots of intramurals. I showed up and played like it would be my last game ever. In graduate school, I discovered running, which led me to my first marathon: the New Jersey Shore Marathon.

I remember the start line well. The guy next to me asked what my goal was. I replied, "It's my first marathon. I would love to do it in four hours or less." He looked me up and down and said, "You'll be lucky to finish in that time." 26.2 miles (in 3:51:48) later, and I made sure he never stepped a foot in front of me. I went on to run seventeen more marathons with a personal record of 2:50:09. I did not know what would be next for me until I read the book *Living with a SEAL* by Jesse Itzler.

I was hooked from the beginning. I wanted to somehow be part of this guy's orbit. I felt that if I could make it there, then I really had willed myself into being an athlete. I filled out the application for Jesse's Hell on the Hill and was quickly turned down. I could have stopped there and said thank you, but I was going to be turning forty that year. I needed this. After a few more email messages, I finally got the answer I wanted. Yes! Hell on the Hill 3 was like no other race/event I have ever been to.

My family and I showed up at Jesse's house the Friday before the race, and I was really nervous. How would I stack up against all these extremely successful people? That night, I told my wife, "No matter what happens on the hill tomorrow, do not pull me off unless I'm dead." I needed to finish, and I had to finish well.

I finished second overall that day, but so much more happened. I realized that to some extent I could now call myself an athlete. Working hard, showing up, and never settling do pay off. That day, Jesse told me I did a hell of a job and that if I wanted, I was invited back to do it again next year. I had entered his orbit, and maybe I was circling the same distance that Pluto orbits our sun, but I was there and I had changed.

The friends I made at Hell on the Hill have been inspirational in all aspects of my life, and I will forever be grateful to Jesse.

I still feel that underdog feeling when I go to events/races. It still pushes me, and the fire to succeed and call myself an athlete still lights.

Nick Newell

Nick Newell is a professional mixed martial arts fighter, a black belt in Brazilian jiu-jitsu, an aspiring Ninja Turtle, and the owner of Fighting Arts Academy. He also fights for Bellator MMA, one of the largest mixed martial arts promotions in the world. He overcame adversity after being born with only one hand and gives back by traveling the country to speak to children with similar challenges. He is currently signed with one of the largest fight leagues in the world: World Series of Fighting. All his fights air live on NBC or NBC Sports Network.

. . . .

So many people have inspired me through the years. I was the first person in my family to play sports so there was no pressure to get involved, but they never discouraged me from trying even though I was born with only one hand. They were all supportive, especially my grandparents, George and Beverly. They have been at every single one of my fights except for when my grandfather was battling cancer. He beat it, and they got right back in the crowd to cheer me on.

Being an inspiration or a role model was not what drove me. It was more about doing the right things, showing kindness and respect to people, working hard, and being true to myself. I followed my heart and did what I loved to do when I was growing up. No one ever told there was something I couldn't do.

From the time I was a kid, baseball pitcher Jim Abbott was my role model. There was no internet then so he was the only other one-handed guy I had ever seen. My grandparents took me to Yankee Stadium, and Jim came out to greet me. Later, when I was on The Dan Patrick Show, Jim called in to tell me he'd seen my fight. It meant the world to me. Seeing all his accomplishments at such a young age made me realize that I was capable of doing anything, and that meant everything.

I tried soccer and then baseball because all my friends played, and Jim Abbott was doing it, too. I was terrible! My first year in baseball, I only got two hits, but I still had fun. I trained when other kids didn't, and the next year I made the all-star team.

I started wrestling because of my neighbor Neil Smith. We would watch WWE together, and one day, Neil said: "I'm going to join the wrestling team." I thought it sounded cool, so I joined, too. Neil only ended up doing it for one year, but I stuck with it and now it's my life. I don't know if I would have ever wrestled had Neil not mentioned it. It's incredible how the smallest things can make such an impact. He changed the course of my life.

One person I don't talk about as often was my friend Pete Bencivenga from the wrestling team. He was a year older and a different kind of guy who marched to his own drum. I always appreciated him for who he was, and he always encouraged me. When I would lose matches and get upset with myself, Pete would tell me that I could quit and stay bad at wrestling forever, or I could choose to train with all the good wrestlers during the summer and get better.

I began training year-round and went from winning only two matches in my freshman year to winning more than twenty during my sophomore year, beating many of the same people to whom I had previously lost. While everyone else was having fun, I was working hard because winning was important to me. I already knew what it was like to lose, and the secret to my success was consistency. Pete said, "Keep showing up and do things better so you can bypass them," so I stayed with it. He suffered a terrible leg injury that required multiple surgeries and later died of medical complications. Pete's encouragement in those early days helped me get where I am today.

My coaches also impacted my life, seeing things in me that I didn't see in myself and believing in me when I doubted my abilities. My first coach, Matt Schoonmaker, pushed me hard, and my current coach, Jeremy Libiszewski, is now one of my best friends, a role model, and a father figure to me.

Another mentor was Abi Mestre, who got into mixed martial arts the same time I did. He taught me to relax and not care so much about what people thought. I was very concerned about what people would think of me if I lost back then. Abi's standard response to most of my statements about being insecure was, "Who cares? Just train." Unfortunately, he lost his life in a motorcycle accident, but he was the key person who gave me confidence.

So my standing O goes to my coaches and family for believing in me, Pete for encouraging me to work hard and be better, Abi for instilling confidence in me, and Jim Abbott, whose quote I live by every day: "Find something you love and go after it with all your heart."

Marques Ogden

Marques Ogden played Division I football at Howard University and then followed his dream and his brother, Jonathan, by getting drafted into the National Football League in 2003. He played for five years as an offensive lineman with the Titans, Bills, Ravens, and Jaguars. In 2007, he started Kayden Premier Enterprises, which quickly grew into a multimillion-dollar construction firm. In 2013, a bad business deal brought things to a halt and taught him the valuable lessons he now shares with others through his work as a speaker, executive coach, and corporate trainer. His book, The Success Cycle, and his online courses and one-on-one coaching promote the benefits of mental toughness over physical limitations.

. . . .

The person who has impacted my life the most was my father, Shirrel Ogden. He was a bank manager for the Federal Home Loan Bank of New York in the D.C. office. He also played football at Howard University, like me, so athletics were always important to him.

My brother was fourteen and I had just turned eight when our parents split up. My father raised two boys by himself while holding down his full-time job and managing to be fully present for my brother and me. We lived in Northeast D.C., and every day we would pile into his small gray Cavalier and drive about forty minutes to Northwest D.C., where he worked and where my brother and I attended school. My dad was 6'4" while I was 5'11" at the time and my brother was already 6'9". Yet somehow, we made it work.

My father sacrificed anything and everything he had, financially and emotionally, and poured his time into us, attending all of my and my brother's games. When my brother went to UCLA, my dad could only attend a few games, but I don't think he missed a home game during my brother's twelve-year career with the Baltimore Ravens. During my high school and college career, my dad was always there, and when I went into the National Football League, he attended every game he could.

To me, it was the epitome of servant leadership, self-sacrifice, and selflessness. He gave everything he had so that his sons could have a better life than he did. He embodied principles that shaped me: a belief in respecting women at all times and self-respect because if you don't respect yourself, how do you expect anyone else to respect you?

He taught us to value our education above athletics. Having athletics become more important than knowledge puts pressure on kids to become incredible athletes and often become the "saving grace" of their families. Kids should be able to do something while parents support and encourage them, but there should never be pressure on them to "save" the family. I see that happen all the time.

There is a life after sports, and if you don't prepare accordingly, everything you've worked for can go out the door when you have no education to fall back on.

My dad also emphasized the importance of surrounding yourself with good people. He believed that who you spend time with is who you become, so we should choose wisely. The beliefs he handed down were so important, particularly when I entered the world of professional athletics.

He passed away in July 2006, eight days after his fifty-seventh birthday. I was twenty-five years old and the one who had encouraged him to have open-heart surgery. He had a condition where the valves around his heart had tightened, and blood flow was restricted. Although he did survive the surgery, he died of complications a few days later.

I spent many years blaming myself for his death, thinking maybe he could have gotten by without the operation. He had convinced me that he would be fine, but it was just too much of a recovery process. It was extremely difficult for me for several years. Then I met my wife, and in 2014, our daughter was born with the same birthday as my dad. I knew had to stop blaming myself and become more positive for her sake. I also realized that without the surgery, his quality of life would have been a struggle. It doesn't get easy; it just gets easier.

I had a dream shortly after the birth of my daughter, and in it, my dad, his best friend, and my uncle were telling me it was time to let go and that my father was okay. I saw him start walking away, and I turned around because I heard my name, but he was gone. Once that happened, I began to stop beating myself up as I had done for many years prior.

My father remains my hero. He taught me all the right things and shaped the man I am today. He made me a teachable person by emphasizing learning. If someone can't grasp the concept of doing whatever it takes to get where you need to go, that person will not be coachable or willing to learn. I lost my first company because I thought I was the best at what I was doing. Little did I realize that although I was good, there was much I didn't know. By the time I realized that, it was too late. Now I teach people how to avoid those kinds of mistakes because I learned from my own.

People do business with people they like, and many forget that. Everyone wants to close the sale today or yesterday, but it doesn't happen that way. It takes time to build good communication, relationships, trust, and respect. I am thankful that I can still lean on the values my father demonstrated and instilled in me every day. It's the kind of legacy everyone should seek to leave behind.

Natalie Pacifico

Natalie Pacifico has dedicated the past ten years to hiring, managing, and recruiting for multiple global Fortune 500 companies. She has led searches for high-level executives at organizations that understand the return on investment when they hire exceptional leaders. She has developed a unique perspective on the factors that dramatically influence organizational culture, which include diversity, equality, and investments in their people. She is passionate about making a path for women leaders to invest in developing our next generation of young talent and gaining more exposure for nonprofit organizations to directly impact the lives of under-represented people, who deserve a chance to thrive.

. . . .

I'm humbled with gratitude to contribute to the exceptional and beautiful spirit that exists in the chapters of *Standing O!*

For all who read these incredibly inspiring stories, I hope the same spark ignites a powerful flame in some capacity as it has for me personally.

I'm forever indebted to friends, family members, and a few mentors who've become legendary giants. And there are many others I've admired for what they've stood for. There are so many teachers of lessons I frequently reflect on. I've been a silent collector and lucky to bear witness to several stories and experiences, each worthy of a memoir.

In my soul, there exist some invisible tattoos inscribed with a few powerful messages and some important lessons I hope to share with others:

- Life is love, and love is life.

- "Passion and persistence are what matter. Dreams are achievable and you can make your fantasy come true, but there are no shortcuts. Nothing happens without hard work." —Diane Von Furstenburg
- "In wisdom gathered over time, I've found that every experience is a form of exploration." —Ansel Adams

- "No man has the right to dictate what other men should perceive, create, or produce, but all should be encouraged to reveal themselves, their perceptions, and emotions, and to build confidence in the creative spirit." —Ansel Adams

- "Nothing is more important than empathy for another human being's suffering. Nothing. Not a career, not wealth, not intelligence, certainly not status. We have to feel for one another if we're going to survive with dignity." —Audrey Hepburn

- "The past, I think, has helped me appreciate the present, and I don't want to spoil any of it by fretting about the future." —Audrey Hepburn

- Every day of life is truly precious. Every sunrise, sunset, and fleeting moment happens for a reason. Be present and appreciate the little things.

- "Travel changes you. As you move through this life and this world, you change things slightly, you leave marks behind, however small. And in return, life—and travel—leaves marks on you." —Anthony Bourdain

- Wherever you can open a door, look someone in the eyes, express gratitude, or be a force to help people in some capacity, do it.

- Be unapologetically brave for everything you stand for. Make your voice heard, never compromise your beliefs, and have dignity to respect the compass in your own heart. Life's a journey. Chart your own course.

Rick Peterson

As a pitching coach with the New York Mets, Oakland A's, and Milwaukee Brewers, Rick Peterson has coached Hall of Famers like Pedro Martinez, Tom Glavine, Trevor Hoffman, and Roy Halladay. Peterson is well-known as a pioneer in combining saber metrics, bio-mechanics, and predictive analysis to keep pitchers healthy and reduce injury. His track record on the field has been chronicled in Michael Lewis's bestseller Moneyball *and John Feinstein's* Living on the Black. *Peterson frequently appears on national radio and TV shows and is a sought-after keynote speaker and business leadership coach. He is the co-author of the award-winning book* Crunch Time: How to Be Your Best When It Matters Most.

. . . .

My dad, Pete Peterson, was my hero. Throughout my life, I always viewed him as my mentor, friend, and hero. He's in the Hall of Fame at Rutgers University and played for the Pittsburgh Pirates. He caught the last games at Ebbets Field and the Polo Grounds. After a collision at home plate that resulted in a broken arm, my dad left the field and began his managing career with the Pirates. He managed throughout the minor leagues, and after many years, he went to the front office and became the general manager for the Pirates and the New York Yankees.

The highlight of his career was being the architect for the 1979 World Series "We are Family" team. What an amazing experience to witness the thrill of winning the World Series! Seeing the champagne showers, the parades, and the city of Pittsburgh on fire with celebration. Imagine being a twenty-five-year-old just beginning your coaching career with the Pirates and we win the World Series—and your dad is the GM! Of course, my dad became an even bigger hero for me then.

Looking back, I realize that what made him my hero was not his baseball accomplishments. It was how he treated people. I think I was two years old when I first put on a baseball uniform. Throughout my life, every time I put a uniform on, the feeling is pure magic. I would travel with my dad to the minor league stadiums in the Carolinas, where he managed. I watched how he interacted with the players and how he always treated them with respect. He would say, "Be fair and do the right thing." This became his motto.

During the 1960s, the Pirates had more black and Latin American players than any other team in baseball. The way he was able to bring this diverse team together at a time when the civil rights movement was raging was just incredible. When the team was traveling to games, Dad would stop the bus and go into a restaurant to make sure that they would feed everyone. In those days, many restaurants in the South wouldn't serve blacks and Latinos. I saw how difficult it was for those players and how my dad was there to nurture them in their careers and lives. He was all about fairness and gratitude, and I saw that firsthand.

It was a difficult time for me, too, because I attended three schools every year. I would start the school year in New Jersey, then I would go to a school where spring training was, and then I'd finish the year at a school in the Carolinas. Dad was always concerned about me being able to handle the travel. From time to time, I'd struggle with understanding the southern accents.

Many times I felt like a minority as well. I didn't talk or dress like everyone else, and the kids always made fun of me. In New Jersey, we wore dress pants, collared shirts, and dress shoes to school. In the South, kids wore shorts, t-shirts, and sneakers to school. One year when I was about seven or eight years old, I was selling popcorn and peanuts at the stadium. In those days, the first-base bleachers were for blacks only. As I started to make my way over from the third-base side, the usher stopped me and said: "You can't go there. This is only for colored people." I looked at the chain separating the sections and said, "Everybody likes popcorn and peanuts, right?" I never understood that separation. This was a hard lesson to learn at a young age.

My dad was different. He always made sure that all the guys on his team had clean places to live because the conditions were so poor, especially for the blacks and Latin players. He found local restaurants where they could eat and be treated well. The south was tough in those days, but

Dad constantly demonstrated how to treat everyone with equality. No one was better than anyone else. Someone once asked him about the Hall of Fame humanitarian Roberto Clemente, and Dad responded that Roberto put his pants on the same way as the rest of us, one leg at a time. This past year, my eighty-nine-year-old dad came down with a nasty virus, and I had the opportunity to be with him every day for a month. We got to share all our favorite baseball stories and laugh about our lives and careers. I was able to tell him what he meant to me. We got to express the love and gratitude that we had for each other. So when he passed away a few weeks later, I felt a deep sense of gratitude that we had had that time together.

A few weeks ago, the Pittsburgh Pirates had a forty-year reunion of the 1979 World Series team, "We are Family." They paid tribute to my dad at the stadium, and I got to represent him on the field. Wow, that was way too cool! And then I heard stories from players like Dave Parker and Teke Tekulve about how my dad made a difference in their lives, too.

My dad taught me that what adds quality to a person's life is making a difference in someone else's. I was truly blessed to play professional baseball, and when I got into coaching, this became my motto as well. Every day, I try to live this, thanks to him.

So, Dad, this standing O is for you!

Kyle Porter

Kyle Porter is founder and CEO of SalesLoft, which creates sales engagement software to help companies boost pipeline and transform teams into modern sales organizations. The Technology Association of Georgia recognized the company as one of the top 10 most innovative companies in the state, and Porter was named TiE's up-and-coming entrepreneur of the year and the Metro Atlanta Chamber of Commerce's businessperson of the year in 2014. As a champion for organizational health and the Atlanta technology ecosystem, he is dedicated to helping SalesLoft's employees accomplish their goals and dreams. He speaks at national conferences on the topic of leadership and blogs at kyleporter.net.

. . . .

Stomping down the back staircase of my fraternity house one day in 1998, I glanced up at the billboard where we posted important events. Right next to the party announcements for "Beer Mug Wednesday" and "Toga Party Friday," I saw a note that read "JOB—$ 10.00 per hour" with a phone number. Out of sheer curiosity, I called, and a gentleman answered who identified himself as the live-in nurse for Dr. John B. Cutler. I learned John was a benefactor to Georgia Tech and a quadriplegic. He was looking for a college student who would come by a few days a week to care for him. I learned one of my graduating fraternity brothers had been visiting John for years, so I decided to try it out.

I'll never forget the first time I met John. Here was a gentleman who had been hit head-on when someone swerved into his robin's egg-blue Jaguar in the 1970s, leaving him paralyzed and under the full-time care of a live-in nurse. But what stood out was the language he used, his constant ear-to-ear smile, and most importantly, how he built others up.

I'd later understand John to be a renaissance man. He was an artist, poet, reader, writer, and lover of classical music, business, port wine, and whiskey. Over the next four years, I spent three or four days a week with him. I would move him around in his bed and cook for him.

He walked me through the timeline of fine art and classical music. We watched old movies from the 1940s and '50s and cherished the dialogue and character development together. We read poetry and discussed the political climate, dating, and relationships. I would even help him get his menthol cigarettes onto a device he had on his wrist so he could smoke. We enjoyed three-martini lunches, and we talked about amazing things in life.

With John, my mind expanded, and I matured by decades in those four short years. John met my family and a handful of my friends. My sister will never forget the day she met him. She poured him a glass of port, and he called her charming. John gave me one of the neatest compliments I ever received. He told me that if I were a stock, he would invest in me, and it meant the world to me. The funny thing is, there were eight of us from the fraternity assisting John, and we all thought we were his favorite! He made each of us feel very special and worthy.

I let him into my life, and we built a strong relationship during some of my most critical and vital years. I would come in bummed about school or struggling with relationships, and John would be grinning ear to ear, just happy to see me and excited about life, learning, growing, and developing. Here was a man who once was in Fence Club with George Bush at Yale, yet even though he'd spent the last thirty years in a wheelchair, he was able to expand his potential every single day.

He taught me to love shellfish and oysters in particular since he was an oyster connoisseur. He went on a North Atlantic seafood cruise to Prince Edwards Island. He had some chemical deficiencies in his body and poor circulation, and he passed away during that trip. He was in his late seventies and was happy as can be.

My wife never got to meet John, but I believe that had she and I met before I knew him, I would have been a different person and we might not have had the same spark. I came in a young man who was rough around the edges and left a well-rounded gentleman.

Most importantly, John taught me "Glass Half Full." It's not about being a Pollyanna or seeing life through rose-colored glasses. The sun doesn't always shine. You have to take everything—the good, bad, and ugly— into full perspective and choose a positive path forward. I've made "Glass Half Full " one of our core values at SalesLoft. Nearly 500 Lofters operate every day under our core values, including "Glass Half Full." John lives on by having impacted not only me, but all the people in my organization, and I will always be grateful.

Caroline Pugh

Caroline Pugh founded Oya Partners in 2019 to work with philanthropists, foundations, and the private sector on a range of issues, including health care, technology, next-generation philanthropy, and leadership. She is a board member and senior advisor to the Mandela Institute for Humanity, which was founded by activist and humanitarian Ndaba Mandela to build on the legacy of his grandfather, Nelson Mandela. She is also an advisor and community leader for Prime Chief of Staff, which provides research, resources, and opportunities for chiefs of staff and CEOs in the private and public sectors. She was recently included on Entrepreneur *magazine's list of top female entrepreneurs to watch.*

. . . .

Having lived in five countries as a child, I was exposed to many cultures and became accepting of new ways of thinking and different ways of doing things. My passion has always been to be the connective tissue behind people and organizations and in everything I do. In 2018, I had the opportunity to meet Ndaba Mandela, Nelson Mandela's grandson, and help him organize a local event as part of his U.S. book launch and tour. I had lived in South Africa as a child, so I was excited to meet him and thrilled by the opportunity to collaborate.

Ndaba's book, Going to the Mountain: Life Lessons from my Grandfather, Nelson Mandela, was a striking narrative that told the story of how Ndaba grew up in the ghettos of Soweto in Johannesburg, then transitioned to living with his grandfather in the presidential estate at the age of eleven, just years after Nelson Mandela's release from prison. What was unique about Ndaba's book was that it was told through the eyes of a grandchild. I later learned that he intentionally chose to share a perspective of his grandfather that had not been shared before.

I continued to help Ndaba with other U.S. initiatives and became an advisor to his South Africa-based foundation, Africa Rising. It has a program called 100 Mandelas, which seeks the next generation of young people willing to carry forth Nelson Mandela's core values and provides the tools and skills they need to be successful leaders. As I worked with Ndaba, it became evident that he has a love for children and young people. I admire his passion for mentorship and his understanding that it's important to inspire and give young people the confidence to think big.

We recently formed his U.S. nonprofit, the Mandela Institute for Humanity, as an extension of his work in Africa, with an added focus of the eradication of HIV/AIDs. The disease has ravaged his country and taken the lives of 35 million people worldwide. Sub-Saharan Africa remains the most severely affected, with nearly one in every twenty-five adults living with HIV, and the region accounts for nearly 70 percent of the people living with HIV worldwide.

In 2005, Nelson Mandela publicly acknowledged that his eldest son had died of the disease and called on the world to end the epidemic. Ndaba is determined to complete his grandfather's wish by bringing an end to AIDS by 2030.

As the only person raised by Nelson Mandela, Ndaba shares a lot of traits with his grandfather. The first thing that struck me about Ndaba was his speaking ability. He can walk into any room, no matter how big or small, and command the attention of each audience member. His conviction and passion are infectious. The ability to strike a balance between being confident, authentic, and humble is difficult for most people, but for Ndaba, it comes naturally, as it did for his grandfather.

Ndaba once shared with me what he believes was his grandfather's greatest trait: "Most people admired my grandfather for his ability to forgive. However, what I admired most about him was that he stayed true to his values the entirety of his life. His core values were to treat everyone with respect and dignity. Whether it was a president at our home or our cook, he would treat everyone exactly the same."

This point really resonated with me as I reflected on how many people I know who I can honestly say have lived up to their values their whole lives. My parents were the only people who came to mind.

As I got to know Ndaba, I soon realized that he carries those same values. He doesn't judge anyone, he is always open to other people's opinions and thoughts no matter how different they are from his own, and he is fair.

In a world where we are quick to judge and place a title and hierarchy on people, whether subconsciously or consciously, it's critical to remember that we are all human. His determination, messaging, and mindset inspire me to think about how I can take one step in that same direction each day and live a life where I stay true to my core values and mission.

Being able to work with people you may not agree with and maintain a dialogue across boundaries are abilities that are lacking today. Nelson Mandela did it in prison by speaking Afrikaans, the "opposing language," and wooing guard after guard. Ndaba has the same gift. People feel understood by him and want to take action alongside him as a result. He wants the world to think about how much more productive and successful we could be as a society if we bridged our gaps and worked together.

Ndaba also reminds young people that we all have a responsibility in our communities and globally to make an active contribution. A lot of people believe that to make an impact, you need to do something grand, donate a lot of money, or start an initiative of your own. However, when you start taking little steps to help, there's a cascading effect. You talk about it with your friends and within your community, and it inspires other people. Because of the social environment we live in today, that message gets shared very quickly.

Africa was a land of abundance before it was heavily colonized. It is time to make it prosperous once again, led by its own people and on a level playing field with the rest of the world. Ndaba experienced firsthand how his life shifted once he had a strong foundation, mentorship, and access to opportunity. He wants all young Africans to have the same opportunity to become leaders.

What would the world look like without HIV/AIDS? How would humanity improve or alter with a new generation of young, motivated leaders working for positive change? What would humanity be like if there were a hundred, a thousand, or a million Mandelas?

My mission now is to uncover the answers to these questions by working alongside leaders like Ndaba. Together, we can achieve anything.

Diane Ristau

Diane Ristau is vice president of recruitment at SomethingNew, where she works on advancing people's career dreams and bringing the best talent to organizations across the globe. Her positive impact extends from talent acquisition to employee learning and development as she partners with leaders to build strong, productive teams and work cultures. Her expertise includes comprehensive talent management services that support organizations in maximizing programs and processes and improving the performance of individuals and teams. She speaks often at national conferences, providing insight and inspiration to company leaders. She is also actively involved in her community and supports multiple nonprofit organizations with her time and talents.

. . . .

Being given the opportunity to tell this woman's story warms my heart. Every time I think of her, hear her laugh in my memories (which was somewhat of a cackle when she thought something was really funny), or picture her standing in her driveway waving to us as we drive away, I have to smile to myself. I always wish I had more time with her. More time to let her way of approaching life influence how I approach life. More time for my kids to know someone who lived simply, humbly, and with love. More time to hear her stories of how she lived through so many hardships, which made the many good times that much sweeter and ones she truly treasured.

Elizabeth Epp Dick lived her whole life in southern Minnesota to the full age of ninety-three, keeping her independence and living in her home until God called her to her forever home. But it's not living to her old age that was impressive, it was how she lived her life when she easily could have been bitter and seen the difficulties of life instead of the blessings.

Elizabeth, now the middle name of my older daughter, was my Grandma. She loved my Grandpa, to whom she was married for sixty-four years. He was a loving, kind, and humble man who always made me laugh, swung me on his foot when his leg was crossed over the other, and occasionally stuttered from being forced at a young age to use his right hand instead of his left. His stutter would come when he prayed before our meals, but he would often be the one to pray anyway. After he passed, Grandma would say the prayer so sweetly, knowing she was talking to a best friend. My grandfather was the owner of a shoe repair shop, and they did not have a lot of money. But God always provided for them, and they were content.

Grandma loved to have people over and cook simple but wonderful German and American food for them. I learned to drink coffee at her house, stirring in a spoonful of ice cream that she served with her warm, homemade apple pie.

My grandparents had three children together, the oldest being my mom, followed by two boys. I'm told that Grandma was always there for them, welcoming them home from school, teaching them Bible verses, going to their games, and mending their clothes.

One might think she had a pleasant childhood to be such a loving person, but that is one of the reasons why I give her a standing O. She endured a lot and didn't let it jade her.

Before Elizabeth turned two, her mother fell ill and died. Elizabeth went to live with relatives because her father couldn't take care of both her and a farm. When he remarried, she and her siblings moved back to the farm. Sadly, the second wife died when Elizabeth was nine. Men, especially farmers, relied on a wife to tend to the family, and so her father married a third time. Tragically, he died when Elizabeth was twelve, and her brother Sammy (eleven) died of scarlet fever three years later. Their stepmother was not a loving person and rarely left her bedroom, causing Grandma's older sister, Sue, to take on the role of mother. Eventually, their stepmother kicked Sue out of the house. This was heartbreaking for Grandma, who loved her older sister very much. The farm was sold, and the children moved in with relatives or their stepmother.

Elizabeth had courage, strength, and faith, and she and half-sister, Clara, rented an apartment and became caretakers of their two younger brothers, Reuben and Henry. The two older brothers moved away. This was a difficult time for all, but the apartment was filled with love. After she married my Grandpa, she continued raising her younger brother Reuben while Sue took in Henry and raised him. A highlight of this time was watching Reuben and Henry play on the same basketball team, winning the state tournament in 1939.

I can still smell my grandmother's house, see the green carpet, hear the creek of the old wooden doors, and see her pretty smile, which would often result in water-filled eyes. She hated to see our visits end, especially after Grandpa died. But she never complained. She just hugged us goodbye and waved from her driveway as we left for the three-and-a-half hour drive home. Or if it was winter, she'd wave from the doorway. When I called her on the phone (which wasn't often before cell phones), she was always easy to talk to, which was funny because she seemed to live in a completely different world from mine. She could talk about the Minnesota Twins or Vikings game the day before and always wanted to know how I was doing.

She was sharp and witty but never mean or sarcastic. I always saw her being kind to others. She spent her time volunteering at the local thrift shop, at church, and at many community events. She taught me how to make piroshki (fruit pockets). She would make hundreds at a time for various fundraisers, even though she did not have a lot of funds herself. After she worked long hours to prepare Thanksgiving, Christmas, or Easter dinners, she would never sit at the table with the family, maybe because the table was packed with the family she loved but probably because she was more concerned about us than herself. She'd sit off to the side and eat at the desk in the dining room, often after the food was no longer hot. Sometimes I'd join her. I wish I'd joined her every time.

She was the last surviving member of her family. But she did more than survive. She thrived—simply, humbly, and with joy.

My grandparents' generation is often referred to as the Greatest Generation because of their ability to live contentedly without. I saw this reflected in both my grandparents and is a quality I hope influences me more as I grow older.

My grandmother lived out her faith through her humility and kindness, always putting others before herself. She gave of her time and gave of her food. She also was dedicated in prayer. One of the greatest blessings I received from her was knowing she prayed for me every day. That was powerful! I am blessed to have a mom, Elizabeth's daughter, who continues in prayer for me today.

Jaime Diglio, president of SomethingNew, asked me awhile back what my favorite quote or saying is. I shared the following: It's not what happens that matters most, it's how you choose to respond. My grandmother, Elizabeth Epp Dick, demonstrated this fully. We all have choices, and our circumstances do not need to define our attitude. Faith in a loving Jesus who had a plan for her life is what gave her the strength to keep joy and kindness in her heart. She did not let her circumstances shape her. She chose kindness, humility, and servanthood. For that and for the impact she had on my life, I give her a standing O!

Ron Rosansky

Ron Rosansky is a lifetime learner with a primary interest in leadership and culture. He is co-founder and CEO of Fidelus Technologies and co-founder of Akkadian Labs. Both are innovative companies on a mission to change how we communicate in the workplace. He enjoys going on adventures that include hiking Mt. Kilimanjaro and the Annapurna Circuit; motorcycling through the U.S., Colombia, and the western Himalayas; and sailing in various parts of the world. He will be participating in his first Ironman Triathlon in 2020 and hopes to sail around the world someday.

. . . .

Thank you, Scott, for having the vision for this book and to all the past contributors for sharing your intimate stories and life lessons.

I am fortunate and grateful to have amazing people in my life. They include my parents, siblings, close friends, teammates, clients, and my mentor. I am a product of these relationships, associated experiences, and the lessons I continue to learn from them. They continue to teach me about hard work, persistence, humility, and generosity.

My father, Martin, was born in Brooklyn and was the son of a house painter. After graduating from Brooklyn Polytech with a master's degree in mechanical engineering, he took a job at a large chemical company before becoming an entrepreneur. Although he didn't receive the best grades, he taught me that there is no substitute for hard work. Regardless of his accomplishments, Dad was always humble and generous with those around him. He taught me countless lessons about life and business and to never, ever give up. I've admired him for as long as I can remember, and he still amazes me. I continue to seek his advice and am grateful for his guidance and our friendship.

When I was four years old, my mother, Marcia, found herself divorced and needed to change her original plans of being a stay-at-home mom. She put herself through school, got a full-time job, and eventually started a small staffing company. Throughout that transition, she never complained or said a negative word about anyone. She always welcomed friends to Friday night dinners after rushing home from work. Mom showed me that women are capable of anything men are and taught me the importance of hard work and generosity. At seventy-two, she met her now significant other, Shelly. Shelly began supporting his parents at the age of eighteen, was a hard worker throughout his life, and couldn't be more kind and generous to those around him.

At the age of seven, I was lucky to gain an amazing stepmother, Diana, also known affectionately as M2. Diana was as kind and generous to my brother, my sister, and me as she was to her own children. She always said that "life is not a dress rehearsal." It's a phrase I still think about today to remind me that tomorrow is not a guarantee.

My siblings humbled me and set an example of hard work, persistence, and generosity. After kicking my butt throughout my childhood, my brothers Larry, Darin, and Andrew became lawyers and worked tirelessly to become successful. My sisters Cheryl and Tammy are incredible, generous, and loving moms. Following surgery for a burst appendix and a close call with death, my sisters were the first ones there. After a nine-day hospital stay, Larry took care of me for two weeks while I recovered. I will never forget those moments.

I met my closest friends in college. Marek, born in eastern Europe, was the valedictorian of our undergraduate program and his master's program. He came to the U.S. when he was sixteen and demonstrated what hard work and focus can lead to. He is now one of the top private equity professionals in the world.

Pat is a natural leader. He started working at a bank while attending college and quickly rose through the leadership ranks. At forty-three, he is now responsible for more than 400 financial advisors at one of largest banks in the world.

Anthony and Evan are fellow entrepreneurs. Anthony's company fabricates and installs high-end stone in some of the most prestigious restaurants and buildings in New York City. Evan owns and runs a hot donut startup and is working diligently to make it one of the best—move over Dunkin'. Their achievements continue to set an example for what can be accomplished through hard work and persistence.

Our company, Fidelus, would not be here today if not for the generosity of a client and one of my closest friends. Dierk was hired by a 160-year-old New York City law firm after 9/11 and tasked with rebuilding their information technology infrastructure. A few weeks after I left my second post-college job in 2002, Dierk called and asked if I could help design and rebuild a resilient communications system for the firm. I told him I would need to start a company and find engineers to do the work. Dierk said, "Ron, if you say you can do it, I trust you."

Soon after, Fidelus was born. Dierk was generous enough to give us the opportunity of a lifetime. Over the years, other clients were generous enough to give us opportunities to work with their firms, and I hope we make them proud.

Dierk, Steve, Peter, Curt, Kermit, Will, and Nader—I can't thank you enough.

Some of my most persistent teachers are my teammates at Fidelus, and I learn from them every day. Tom, Don, Eric, Sue, Josh, Anthony, Joe, and others continue to help me grow. For that I am sincerely grateful.

Last and certainly not least is one of the most generous and hardworking people I know, Mike Feiner. He is the former chief people officer at Pepsi and a former leadership and management professor at Columbia Business School. Simply put, no one who has experienced more or is wiser when it comes to corporate leadership. His intuition and insight into people and situations are second to none. Mike sets the precedent for leadership excellence and always reminds me how difficult and important it is to have high leadership standards. He not only shares his time and wisdom with me, he is also very generous with other colleagues and friends.

Thank you all for contributing to the person I am today. I am and will remain eternally grateful.

Brian Scudamore

Brian Scudamore is founder and CEO of O2E Brands—the banner company for 1-800-GOT-JUNK?, WOW 1 DAY PAINTING, You Move Me, and Shack Shine—and is a serial entrepreneur. He is a respected industry leader and speaker who is well-known in the business community for his belief in people and his passion for innovation. His companies have made celebrated appearances on ABC's Nightline, Good Morning America, Dr. Phil, CNN, NBC's Today, The Oprah Winfrey Show, *and CNBC. His story has been featured in* Fortune *magazine,* The New York Times, Huffington Post, *and* The Wall Street Journal, *and he contributes regularly to other noteworthy publications.*

· ·

Greig Clark started a company called College Pro Painters, which he ended up selling for millions of dollars. I had a problem in my business at one point, and although Greig and I had never met, I turned to him in a moment of crisis. Over several calls and several hours, he walked me through what was happening. We determined what the challenges were and what I needed to do to fix them. He was a coach, mentor, and advisor. Amazingly, this person who was almost a total stranger helped and supported me, and as a result, I try to do the same for others.

I had a chance to pay it forward when someone who read my book reached out to me needing help of a different nature. He had read an article about how, when I was in my twenties and early thirties, I suffered from debilitating anxiety and panic attacks that impeded my business and personal life. I ended up getting treatment, medication, and some tools that helped me move past it all. My life is amazing now, but there was a ten-year period where it was tough.

This man was a CEO himself and struggling with the same issues. We spent some time together over a couple of calls, and I got an email message from him a month later expressing immense gratitude and saying that I had changed his life. He went from a nightmare existence plagued with panic attacks to getting the proper treatment to help him overcome them. Now he feels blessed, and his life is so different.

He said that although we had never met, I had taken time out of my busy day to spend with him, guiding him and sharing my experience to allow him to get the support he needed. The lesson here is that we are all human beings on this planet. No matter what's going on in our lives that may be unique and different, we have that in common. Why not support someone who reaches out when you are the one who can provide help? My grandparents taught another excellent example of that kind of humanity. They ran a small army surplus store in San Francisco, and I would "play the game of business" while working the cash register and talking to clients. From about the time I was seven until I was seventeen, I would work in their store over spring breaks or Christmas holidays, and I learned that they truly believed in people.

Employees, customers, and anyone coming in to say hello who would never become a customer were all treated with respect and kindness. Located in the Mission District, the store was not in a nice part of the city. There were a lot of people having challenges. A man came inside in a wheelchair saying one of the tires was flat and asked for money to get it fixed. My grandparents knew he likely let the air out of the tire intentionally, and instead of giving him money, they gave him kindness. They got to know him a little bit; they asked how he was doing and what was going on in his life. They gave him what he really needed, which was love.

They used to have homeless people come in all the time, and I noticed that the shops to the left and right of their store would get continuously robbed, yet it never happened to them. I realized it was because the people who were part of some of the robberies knew they were good-hearted and treated everyone with dignity. The word on the street was not to mess with them, and it was powerful for me to witness.

At our business, it doesn't matter if someone is the vice president of operations or on the phone in the call center, they are equally important and deserve love and respect always.

I often wonder what would happen if the world adopted the philosophy that when someone asks for help, you do your best to give it to them. Another great mentor, Verne Harnish, once said: "You get more if you give." If there is somebody you can help versus ask for help, that's always the best way to start—by sincerely reaching out without any belief that you'll get something back in return.

Reach out and help a whole bunch of people, and one day when you need help yourself, it's going to come back to you. It has never let me down, so why not try to support a stranger?

Crystal Seaver

Crystal Seaver is a fitness trainer by trade and community connector by passion. She has a lust for healthy adventure, runs a lot, and writes a blog that is best described as an open-book life diary. When she is not frequently flying, she calls Charlotte, North Carolina, home and can often be found enjoying a good coffee shop, dog-walking her two fur babies, and soaking up time with family. She's up for the everyday adventure, believes there is a lot of power in movement, and can always be convinced to enjoy a good chocolate chip cookie.

. . . .

Life lessons—there are a lot of them. Sometimes they come from the fact that we didn't know better. Usually it's because we did know better, but we just didn't let it sink in. And once we start living—I mean really living, facing real life head-on—we start feeling and we learn.

My top five life lessons, learned from my sister, are:

- Relationships are paramount.

- There is power in vulnerability.

- Movement is powerful.

- It — whatever it is — will pass.

- We have choices.

Let me share the backstory. It's a long story, but I will keep it short. It centers around drug addiction. Probably not what you expected, right? But from the hardest moments of life, we learn to experience and we dig deep to find gratitude that we know is probably just a little bit clouded. I know what it's like to be a non-addict and love someone who suffers from addiction (recovery period or not). For me, that someone happens to be my younger sister.

If I could rewind time to when we were three and six years old, you would see bright smiles, a carefree life, and a relationship that didn't waiver. And then something changed. For the past ten years, we have been living the addiction battle. You see, addiction isn't individual; it impacts the entire family. I don't like to admit it, but these years were the hardest of my life. You wouldn't know that, though, because masking the lies, the moments of anger, the hurt, and worry—I nailed it, with a smile. Like I said, we know better, we just don't let it fully sink in.

So I pushed the realest parts of life to the back of my mind and smiled. I ran a whole lot, too. But addiction is not a solitary disease, it definitely doesn't go away, and it forever changes your life. We smile, and we push it to the back of our minds (until we can't). Then we feel and we learn. And I will share what I have learned with you.

- **Relationships are paramount.** When you think you may never see a person again, you know just how pivotal a bond is. It shouldn't take something so dramatic for us to recognize that what matters most are the people in our lives. But in my case, maybe it did. People are gold. Put them first, tell them you care, look up from your screen more often, and never give up on someone (even when you want to).

- **There is power in vulnerability.** You can keep it all in, or you can let your guard down, live outside the walls, and share the feelings you are pushing to the back of your mind. It's in this space that we build connection, find strength, and continue to move forward.

- **Movement is powerful.** Endorphins are good for you. I'll leave it at that and let you find the movement that lifts you up.

- **It — whatever it is — will pass.** Bad moments, great moments— they pass. Life comes in phases. Embrace the ebbs and flows. Time passes, things change.

- **We have choices.** Although we can't control the universe (if we could, I certainly wouldn't have experienced what it is like to face addiction), we can choose our response. That response has to keep us moving forward in life, one step at a time. Let's do it with a happy heart, healthy body, and grateful attitude.

Jamie Shanks

Jamie Shanks is CEO of Sales for Life, the leading social selling management, consulting, and training company in the world. He enables millions of sales professionals to move from an analog to a digital selling world, driving revenue and creating growth. He is the bestselling author of SPEAR Selling *and* Social Selling Mastery, *a number one Amazon Hot New Release in sales, and has an MBA in international marketing. A serial entrepreneur, he grew up in rural Canada and has a love of the outdoors and an affinity for his "crazy blazer collection."*

. . . .

I grew up on the edge of the Ottawa Valley, where my parents created a stable, structured, middle-class life for my siblings and me. Mom was a neonatal nurse and Dad a geologist in the oil business who worked on rigs doing exploration. Although I appreciated the comfortable life I enjoyed, I yearned for more.

My father had two friends who significantly impacted me as a teenager. One was a cowboy oil explorer named Emmitt, and the other was a high-rolling stockbroker named Michael. Emmitt worked with my father on the oil rigs. He was a cowboy's cowboy and in 1981 decided to strike out on his own in exploration. He did his best to persuade my father to join him, with no success.

Our family reconnected with Emmitt around 1992, and his life appeared disastrous to me. Some poor oil investments had left him and his family in debt and stretched financially. My parents pointed to this as a cautionary tale of entrepreneurship, but ironically, it didn't faze me.

Dad's other best friend, Michael, was a stockbroker at the Bank of Montreal. I was able to secure a summer job with him during the rise of the 1990s, and he was making money hand over fist. I watched the salespeople doing massive deals and emulated them—walking, talking, and dressing the part.

Around that time, Emmitt's life changed dramatically. New oil endeavors began paying millions of dollars. Suddenly, he owned a horse ranch, collected Porsches, and amassed a fortune. Exposed to great wealth through these two people, I became infatuated with it. I understood that hard work and risk taking could yield great reward.

I finished my master's degree with $60,000 in debt and struggled to find work. My parents supported me for a few years while I lived in Toronto, but eventually, the ultimatum came to get a job or move back home to Ottawa.

I had interviewed several times at a commercial real estate firm that refused to hire me due to my lack of technical sales experience. Desperate to avoid living in my parents' basement, I went back one last time. When the receptionist left, I snuck in and found the CEO's office.

There was Dean Newman on his way out carrying his squash bag. "Who are YOU?" he asked. I quipped, "What? You have interviewed me four or five times. How do you NOT remember who I am?" He told me to walk with him to his club, and for seven blocks, I begged him to hire me. He loved my tenacity and finally hired me as a commissioned sales rep. The dichotomy of the Pareto principle surrounded me: 20 percent of brokers commanded 80 percent of the money. I became successful as Dean took me under his wing, teaching me everything he knew about sales structure and process.

I did the hard things first. Rise early, book meetings and appointments, and build my list. Dean said, "If you can build your pipeline first, all the other things will take care of themselves." He gave me the most valuable skill, which I now teach people in modern digital selling: prospect with confidence. It is the single greatest strength I have from a sales perspective, and it gave me the confidence to build my business from scratch.

I met my current mentor two years ago. Although I ran a multimillion-dollar business, I had not learned the importance of financial operations. After two bad sales months and no retained earnings, I was a half-million dollars in the hole and distraught. I was fortunate to meet Matt Sharrers, CEO of Sales Benchmark Index, and for two years, we had monthly calls.

Matt taught me an executive decision-making framework, separating Jamie the Investor from Jamie the CEO. This framework gave me the conviction to create a vision, set a course, and build a strategy around it. I don't have a single friend who is an entrepreneur, so I seek out entrepreneurial advice whenever I can and invest in myself.

"Caviar on Nachos" is a nickname I got from my friends at university, and it sticks to this day. They said, "Jamie, deep down, you are a plate of nachos who always aspired to have caviar dip on top," and it's true. I grew up a country kid who desired to be better, and I am thankful for my mentors. They shaped my dream of being something bigger than I already am today.

Tibor Shanto

Tibor Shanto is principal at Renbor Sales Solutions Inc. and founder of the Pro-active Prospecting Club. He has been a sales leader for more than twenty-five years, helping companies increase results and sell better. As an execution specialist, he focuses on critical aspects of tactical execution and adoption of sales initiatives. He is the co-author of the award-winning book Shift!: Harness the Trigger Events That Turn Prospects Into Customers. *He is also a columnist for the* Globe and Mail Report on Small Business *and was ranked eighth on a list of the top 30 social salespeople in the world on Forbes.com in 2014.*

. . . .

The minute I was invited to contribute an essay to this book, I knew who I would write about, but his full name escapes me. I remember his first name was Jim, and I want to say his surname was McKnight. Maybe he'll read this and confirm. In the Jewish tradition, there are eight levels of giving or charity, and one of the highest is where neither the giver nor receiver knows the other. Although this isn't exactly the same, I clearly don't fully know who he is, and he likely has no clue of the impact he had on me, but I am forever grateful.

In 1987, I was working for a discount broker in Toronto. Those were heady days, and I was part of the next wave of young studs to have the future by the tail. We didn't miss an opportunity to let anyone and everyone know. We weren't obnoxious or rude but always made everyone aware that "we're here."

A favorite ritual was being wined and dined by representatives of American trading houses who executed our U.S.-traded securities. We were in our late twenties, trying to fit in, very much in the fashion of the day—think Gordon Gekko and his apprentice Bud Fox in the movie *Wall Street*. Don't judge; others went for the big-hair look, but we thought we wanted to be Bud.
So it was that we found ourselves at a high-end Toronto steakhouse, the kind of place the people who were real shakers on Bay Street hung

out after hours. A place to see and be seen. A place that at that age, I could only enjoy on a New York execution house's credit card, which we did to the max.

I left not thinking much of the night. I am not a big drinker, so nothing to worry about there. I did nothing I thought would embarrass me, my mother, or my firm. A few loud jokes, the usual kibitzing, but nothing that stuck with me by the time I got home.

The next morning, I was handed a special order, meaning I had to shop it around to traders at the full-services houses to move the trade. The first place I called was LOM, a renowned Toronto firm. Jim answered the phone, and we talked through the trade. He was ready to take it. Then he asked: "How did you enjoy ACME last night?"

"It was really good, had fun—wait, how did you know I was there?"

"Everyone knew you were there. You were hard to miss." He did add that you represented the whole group, including the out-of-towners. I replayed the evening in my mind. No, nothing goofy, rude, the usual laughs, but everything in line with how we thought young studs and future barons behave. We were not behaving any differently from the other patrons.

Jim went on to tell me that we work in a funny industry that attracts different people. Some were good people working in the industry for the wrong reasons; others were not so good but doing their best and good work. They go through different phases or cycles. "Sometimes they're on top, then they fail, only to do it all over again," Jim said. "You can survive a lot of different challenges and highs if you focus on and protect one thing: your reputation. It's the only thing you have when you come into the business, and if you make sure it is intact throughout your career, you're a success."

Reputation is a funny thing. You can work on it in different ways, but it will always be determined by others. And no matter what your intention is, that determination will always be based on your actions.

Those words have helped shape my thinking. Like many, when presented with something new, I ask: "What's in this for me?" At the same time, I also ask, "How will this impact my reputation?" As a result of what Jim said, I now ask not just about the immediate impact, but: "How will this impact my reputation ten years from now?"

This is not to say that I live an angelic life or will not act in my own best interest. I can prove an argument wrong without destroying the person making it because of my reputation. I can go after a popular bully, be an outcast, and still have my reputation. I can be aggressive without it happening at someone else's expense. You can take advantage of someone else's missteps or mistakes as long as you don't develop a reputation for causing those things.

Andy Shay

Andy Shay recently finished his sixteenth season as the head coach of the Yale Men's Lacrosse Team. He has led the Bulldogs through nine ten-win seasons and been named the Ivy League and ECAC coach of the year. He brought his team to back-to-back appearances in the national title game in 2018 and 2019, giving Yale its first NCAA lacrosse championship in 2018 and runner-up in 2019. Ten straight Ivy League tournament appearances, five Ivy League tournament titles, three regular-season Ivy League championships, and seven NCAA appearances round out his stellar coaching career.

. . . .

A host of people have influenced me in my coaching career. Undeniably, my father was my launching pad. He was a high school basketball coach and also served as district attorney in our town for twenty years. For a long time, I wanted to do those two things. However, once I started coaching, my path was clear, and I abandoned any thought of law school.

Dad was in the Marine Corps after college, and when he put a whistle around his neck, he was a Marine again. His voice was sharp and stern, and his commands would cut through the air like a fist punching you in the chest. He was as concise a teacher as I've ever seen, with total command of his teams, wasting very little time or words as he coached.

As I started in my coaching career, many of my practices were spent trying to imitate him. Today, I'm not sure if I have my own style or if I still resemble his, but whatever it is, it works. I like to think that he would enjoy our practices if he could see them. He stopped coaching in 1982, and dementia has robbed me of an invaluable sounding board as he grew older.

There were other influences along the way for me as well, including but not limited to my high school coaches, my college coach, and my mentors and fellow assistants. Our team has a motto of "O.N.E.," short for "Only Need Everyone," which signifies one team, one more play, one more practice. I believe success starts with the part everyone around us plays in achieving our goals. With that, I have to point to one person who has inspired me more than anyone else: my wife, Sheila.

Sheila is the "head coach" of our family, and she makes it look uncomplicated. She gives me confidence and keeps me grounded. As I've grown and learned over the years, I've come to appreciate the power of humility and the razor's edge between confidence and hubris. Sheila walks that razor-thin line with ease.

As a coach, my best growth moments come from losses when my team and I have an opportunity to check our egos and fortify our weaknesses. Families have losses, too, and sometimes hit significant bumps in the road. We suffered through a house fire that put us out of our home for six months. The collateral emotional damage is difficult to quantify. Unless you have lived through a similar event, you probably wouldn't be able to understand how hard it is.

Coach Sheila was the one stewarding our team through a devastating family loss. While I left to do my job, she rolled up her sleeves and went to work itemizing everything we lost, wrestling with the insurance company daily, and coordinating with our builder to re-create the home we'd had. With little sleep, she did everything our family needed to get back to normalcy. She was grinding for more than half a year with only her family's best interests at heart. She helped our young children feel safe again. It was leadership like I've never seen, and the word inspiring doesn't begin to do it justice.

I am so thankful for the beautiful people I have in my life and for the opportunity to pay it forward daily. I can only hope to be as impactful in other people's lives as Sheila and my father have been in mine.

Claude Silver is an emotional optimist, coach, manager, and mentor. It is her great honor to lead at VaynerMedia as the company's first chief heart officer. She works for 800 humans and is in touch with the heartbeat of every single person in the company. She believes that culture is the heartbeat of an organization, and when the culture is healthy, it lights up an entire system. The CHO position was created to make sure that VaynerMedia's employees have a place they can find a home, and her hope is that she can help employees find new paths to solutions, which in turn creates success for them and VaynerMedia.

· ·

When I think of giving gratitude, my Nana comes to mind. She died almost three years ago at 101 years young. Nana was there the day I was born and remained an integral part of my life until her last days. When I was young, she began to call me Heart, and I reciprocated with the same name. The nicknames stuck, and it was rare that I would call her Nana or she would call me Claude. When we called one another on the phone, we would say "Hi, Heart. It's Heart. How are you?" I never asked her why because intuitively it just made so much sense to me. We loved each other at an exceptional level.

Although my parents are very generous and authentic people who contributed significantly to my life, it was Nana who emotionally raised me, becoming my confidante. She knew all my secrets and everything about me. I may have disbursed certain things to different friends throughout life, but I haven't had one particular vessel other than Nana with whom I feel comfortable placing all my vulnerabilities.

She forged her work ethic from the age of six at her dad's general store in Michigan. She never attended college and later married, having four children. My mom was the oldest, followed by a stillborn baby and then Nana's two sons, one of whom she buried at the age of thirty-three. Outliving a child is not something one could ever prepare for, and although she carried great sorrow and never hid that, she carried a huge flame of life inside her, and this is what everyone was able to see and get close to.

She worked at Saks Fifth Avenue in Los Angeles until she was eighty. The day she retired, we carried her on our shoulders. She had impeccable style and was incredibly elegant. Being in the "schmatta business" surrounded by all the designer clothing was so enjoyable for her. The irony was that she was labeled the "ugly duckling" when she was growing up, which at times created child-like insecurity in her. I wonder if that drove her to develop her inner self and led her to her purpose of loving and serving others.

Nana would go out of her way to make someone's day better. Whenever she paid a cashier, she would say "Thank you so much. Would you do me a favor?" Of course, they would say yes, and she would tell them, "Would you have a nice day? "or "Would you have a peaceful day?" All that mattered to her were people.

When I moved to London, I called her every day to discuss what was going on in my life. Sometimes I would play the mediator between her and my mom, and she would call me her psychologist, although she was mine, too. When I came out many years ago, my mom struggled a bit, and my dad was adorable and asked: "Is it because I taught you how to throw a football?" All Nana said was, "I just want you to be happy. It doesn't matter." It was pretty incredible for a person of her age to be so accepting.

She stayed very active as a hospital volunteer and at her temple, and she still drove until the age of ninety-nine. She was a remarkable human being who was so full of gratitude for life and understood that it is multidimensional, full of sorrow, suffering, pain, joy, and happiness. She chose joy. She was a very spiritual person, cared deeply about her family, and sought out community, sending birthday cards to everyone. Her top five keys to living were: In partnership and marriage, never go to sleep mad at each other; have a lot of sex; choose work that brings you joy; be of service; and never say no to a glass of Crown Royal.

She even kept notes around her house to remind her of how to say things in a "politically correct" way because she'd been born in 1915 and the language we now use for ethnic groups, for instance, is very different.

That's the integrity of someone who cared about being empathetic and respectful in everything she did.

She started to "get old" around age 100. Because I knew she wouldn't live forever, I began to save messages from her on my phone. We had a huge 100th birthday party for her, and during my brother's toast, he asked her what the secret to life was. She said, "I can only tell you that love is the answer. Being in love—and living love—is a wonderful, wonderful thing to be able to say in your life. Love! Love! Love!"

After she died, I realized how lonely I was without her and still am in the way of missing that one person to share everything. I manifest the things she taught me every day of my life. She showed me how to live, with all my warts and imperfections, and she is my inspiration.

When I came to VaynerMedia, Gary Vaynerchuk asked me, "What is it you want to do?" I said, "I only care about the heartbeat of the company, the people." It was the coolest thing to be able to share my job title with Nana. Gary didn't know she called me Heart until that day, so it's all a mitzvah. It was supposed to happen.

When people say to me, "I know you are so busy," I think yes; however, we are all busy around here. I never want to make people feel as though I am too busy for them because I'm not. I would stop the world, and whatever has to happen needs to happen. I can thank my Nana for that. She was the original chief heart officer.

Suzanne Spaner

Suzanne Spaner is a self-starter who needs little direction to be off to the races—literally. She had the desire to raise money for the Arthritis Foundation after growing up with a mother battling rheumatoid arthritis. Without any prior running experience, Spaner trained for the Honolulu Marathon as a Joints in Motion participant and raised $10,000. In the years that followed, she inspired her friends and sister to continue raising funds as participants in the Alaska Marathon/Hike and the Dublin Hike. After working for many years in the hospitality industry, she founded Meeting Matchmakers in 2010. She matches clients with venues worldwide for their meetings.

. . . .

I am very grateful that I am alive today due to the courage of my paternal grandfather. His name was Lazar (Ovadyah Eliezer) Yakobowicz. He journeyed by boat from Poland to Cuba in the early 1930s, leaving behind his parents and siblings on a mission to work and send much-needed money home to them.

My grandfather wasn't the oldest sibling, but he was the only one willing to leave to help the family during the times of the pogroms and ghettos.

Once in Cuba, he worked alongside a tailor and learned that trade. He continued to send money to Poland until he learned that the money wasn't being picked up on the other end. It still breaks my heart to tell this story: Imagine a young man leaving his family and going out on his own to help support them during the most difficult of times then learning that they were all murdered and he would never see them again.

I was not fortunate enough to meet my father's father. A man with courage and fortitude. A man who experienced such tremendous loss. A man who kept this very harrowing time to himself and my grandmother. He didn't want my father to bear the incredible pain of his life. I admire him for his strength and selflessness.

My maternal grandparents repeated these mantras to my sister and me:

- "To thine own self be true, and it must follow, as the night the day, thou canst not then be false to any man." —William Shakespeare

- *Tempus fugit* and *carpe diem* (Latin phrases that mean "time flies" and "seize the day," respectively).

- "If a man does not keep pace with his companions, perhaps it is because he hears a different drummer. Let him step to the music which he hears, however measured or far away." —Henry David Thoreau

What a bold way to live!

Be true to yourself.

Seize the day (every moment/opportunity) because time flies.

March to your own music.

Don't let anyone slow you down.

This is your life, so live it.

Be a role model/guide to others.

Brainstorm.

When all else fails, try again.

Ask for help.

There may be an idea you haven't thought of yet.

Don't be afraid.

Stay positive.

I strive to live my life this way every day, thanks to the lessons my grandparents taught me.

Nicholas Spike

Nicholas Spike is a New Yorker by birth, but after growing up in Florence, Italy, he is a Fiorentino at heart. He has worked in sales for the New York Jets, the New Jersey Devils, and the Barclays Center. He now runs a sales team at Confirmed360 that provides unique entertainment experiences to clients around the world. He has written various articles on the artist Richard Anuszkiewicz and is co-author of Anuskiewicz: Paintings and Sculptures 1945-2001. *He also collaborated with his father, art historian John T. Spike, to write the* catalogue raisonné *of the paintings of Gregorio Preti (1603-1672).*

. . . .

Scott MacGregor kindly (like anything he does) asked me to write an essay for the first edition of *Standing O!* and I never got around to it. I tend to procrastinate, and somehow it never made my priority to-do list. What a fool! Seeing the success of the incredible *Standing O!* community and reading their awesome words made me realize my mistake, and I regretted not getting it done for Scott. But he is an incredible man and has given me a second opportunity. For that and everything else he does for his colleagues, clients, friends, and family, he gets my first standing O.

Recognizing one amazing person in my life seemed too small when there are so many people who have shaped me. Since this isn't an award ceremony, I won't thank God first (or will I?), but my spiritual belief has been an unseen support column in my life. My small family (Dad, Mom, Aunt Jo, and two grandparents) raised me wonderfully, which I now carry into my own family life (*besos a Marce y Santiago*). All these loved ones get a standing O.

Teachers do not get enough credit in today's world. They are paid too little, work long hours, have insane amounts of patience, and are not appreciated. Every single day, teachers shape future generations. This generation seems to care, at least based on social media feeds, about the environment, recycling, women's rights, animal extinctions, poverty, and education. Yet I know two teachers—and there are many more—who at the beginning of every school year have to buy all the supplies needed in their classrooms for their students because the school won't pay and the kids can't afford to. That is wild! All teachers get a standing O.

That being said, three specific teachers changed my life. I was born with a discoid meniscus in my left knee and never walked properly. I had surgery to fix it, and although my body healed, my mind never trusted that knee. I've always loved sports but never thought I could be an athlete. My middle-school gym teacher, Professore Orlandi, only saw a big American kid (I grew up in Florence, Italy) and put me to work. No excuses, no BS, just intense training and trying every single sport out there. Thanks to him I got over my "injury" and have enjoyed a lifetime of playing and now working in sports. Professore Orlandi gets a standing O.

Although I was never a great student, I wasn't that bad either. I just didn't find reading or writing very enjoyable. My high-school freshman English teacher, Mr. John Pitonzo, changed that. He made reading books an adventure, and writing became creating my own story that could change the minds of others. Because of him, I love reading and have published three books and a few essays, including this one. Mr. Pitonzo gets a standing O.

Going to college in the USA was awesome, an experience unlike any other that many consider the best four years of their lives. Moving from Florence to State College, Pennsylvania, was exciting, scary, new, strange, and many other emotions all at the same time, all happening to a free-from-parental-supervision eighteen-year-old. It took some adjusting—not to the partying, but to the studying and maturing part. It wasn't until I enrolled in Mike Poorman's sports journalism class that I grasped the importance of taking advantage of everything those amazing four years had to offer. His natural, engaging teaching style encouraged our class to explore our boundaries and learn about new sports and new locations on campus. From that class, I got my first job in sports and haven't looked back. Mr. Poorman gets a standing O.

My hope is that others who read this essay will think about all the teachers who influenced their lives. Teachers are an essential fabric to our world, and giving our appreciation seems the least we can do. Obviously, there are many more people I'd like to stand up and applaud, but that seems enough for now. Hopefully, Scott will deem me worthy of writing another essay for another edition. I know I will never turn him down again.

Katey Stone

Katey Stone is the Landry Family Head Coach for the Harvard Women's Ice Hockey Team. She has amassed 476 victories throughout her coaching career and will embark on her twenty-fifth season at the helm in 2019-2020. She has coached eleven Olympians and received numerous honors, including eight Ivy League championships, seven ECAC regular season titles, and six tournament championships. She appeared on the New England Hockey Journal's *list of the top 50 most influential people in New England hockey. Her achievements on and off the ice earned her an NCAA Silver Anniversary Award and induction into the University of New Hampshire's Athletics Hall of Fame.*

. . . .

I come from a family of coaches, so it's like our family business. My dad was an athletic director and coached football and baseball at Taft. Growing up in that environment was a fantastic opportunity for us, and athletics were a part of our daily lives.

I loved competing at the high school and college levels, so coaching came naturally to me. It allows me to stay competitive and keeps the fire in my belly. I had some excellent coaches and learned what I liked and what I wanted to leave. My lacrosse coach at the University of New Hampshire, Marge Anderson, was a tremendous influence on me and shaped much of who I am as a coach today. With Marge, I took more than I ever left. She knew how to do it right.

Marge had scoliosis and had to overcome a lot as a young person to become an incredible athlete. She had strong resilience and perseverance and was a two-sport star: All American at the University of Massachusetts and a national team player in lacrosse. It was awesome to play sports with a coach who was better than all of us. Marge created a team environment that was healthy and fun. She mastered the art of fostering positive rivalries among her players and our competitors. We were always prepared and often exceeded our team's talent expectations because of the great dynamic she created within the team, which was based on loyalty to one another and trust.

Marge also made highly competitive athletics fun and always wrapped some sort of bonding experience into everything we did. We would have an Easter egg hunt as part of our pregame preparation with a story at the end to tie it all together. She had an organic way of getting the most out of her players by never letting us settle. Extraordinarily demanding but very respectful, she challenged us in a constructive, positive way. I genuinely loved going to practice, and although it was hard, it was incredibly satisfying.

Marge and I developed a friendship, and when we traveled, I would always sit with her so I could absorb as much as possible. She was such an enjoyable person to be around, and that made me want to take in everything she had to share. Although she had a tremendous amount of pressure and responsibility, still being a competitive athlete herself, she was able to balance her personal and professional lives while staying present for her athletes. That was a gift I always appreciated, and I try to emulate it with my own coaching style.

It's essential for me to still do the things that I expect the kids to do on the ice. I may not be able to do the drills at the same pace or intensity as before, but being engaged with my team and demonstrating the drills gives me credibility. There's nothing I am asking them to do that I haven't already done. It's important to me that the players understand I have been there before and know what it's like. Greater trust builds, and they know I am trying to help guide them toward success.

I often joke with my players that I was either going to be a lawyer or a coach. I didn't have the memory to be a lawyer, so coach it was, and I wouldn't have it any other way!

Mike Teixeira

Mike Teixeira is the founder of DECK, a presentation agency. Growing up in an immigrant household, he realized the importance of communication. His knack for storytelling was forged in the theater, first in an educational setting and then in Los Angeles. He filled in the gaps with video production, branding, and design, which evolved into creative direction. His background and experience led him to become a presentation expert, and he has put his corporate communications skills and theater degree to work. The award-winning results have helped big companies—including Timberland, CTI, and Spotify—bridge their communication gaps.

. . . .

I remember it being a warm day. I was pulling weeds. Sweat dripped from my temples as I struggled to get to the root of the next weed and pull it out whole. I heard loud speaking and, curious, got up and walked toward the sound. I came around the corner of the house and stopped a few feet behind my dad. I was no older than thirteen—not confident enough to speak up as my dad was being yelled at by the homeowner.

We were landscapers, and the owner wasn't angry exactly but speaking loudly as people sometimes do, hoping the increased volume would bridge a language gap. He looked at my father with a mixture of annoyance and pity. He wanted my dad to understand where a bush was to be planted. As I stood there, I thought about the size of the gap between those two men—not of space, but of perception. This man had no idea that my dad was extremely intelligent, a shrewd entrepreneur, a lover of poetry and music, and an amazing storyteller. All he could see was an immigrant who didn't speak perfect English.

That moment struck a chord deep within me. I've spent my whole life trying to figure out how to bridge the gap between the information we hold inside and the comprehension of the people we share information with. The causes of that gap can be many: language, technical expertise, length of experience, acronyms, etc. Through trial and error, I've learned a few ways to shorten that gap:

- **Empathy**—Who are you sharing information with? If you can put yourself in their shoes and try to understand what they need from the information you are sharing, you've won half the battle. Nurturing this ability requires a new way of showing up for work—not behind a business façade, but present and attuned to your emotions and those of the people around you.

- **Focus**—Once you understand your audience's goals (e.g., to learn, to make a decision, to laugh), you have to keep that goal in your sights always. Don't be tempted by distractions, such as being clever, showing off your background or depth of knowledge, being liked. Instead, help the people in your audience reach their goals and humble yourself to the task of being in their service.

- **Stories**—We are wired to learn through stories. Early humans sat huddled near the fire listening to stories. We learned where to hunt, what to fear, what to ignore through those stories. That ingrained habit has been lodged into our evolutionary DNA over thousands of years. Maybe we took a break from stories in business for a short time through the industrial revolutions. But that 200-year span barely made a dent in eliminating our ability and need to learn through this method. However, it is a tricky tactic to master if you're using it for business purposes. A story has to be aligned with the audience's needs and your goals.

Today, we can see that we've let our natural communication abilities atrophy. But I know that all it takes is striking the flint of insights to fan the fires of connection with us.

I'm grateful that I grew up in an immigrant household. It made me acutely aware of communication gaps, and I'm especially grateful to have a dad who took every opportunity to punctuate any issue with a relevant story.

Brendan Thompson

Brendan Thompson is an entrepreneur and endurance athlete. He is the co-founder of 50 Strong, a sporting goods and lifestyle brand that designs and manufactures products that help consumers live happier, healthier lives. 50 Strong products are sold in retail locations nationwide, and the brand has been featured in Forbes, Bloomberg, Fox Business, Rachael Ray Show, *and a Walmart TV campaign. To date, he has completed three 29029 Everesting events and multiple marathons and triathlons.*

. . . .

Life lessons have come in many forms throughout my life. Some have been learned through failure, others through victory, and yet others have come through conversation with and observation of two of the most important people in my life: my mom and my wife.

I was one of four very active children so our house was a beautiful symphony of chaos. In the center of the madness was a strong, calm, reassuring rock—Eileen Lavelle. My mom was a full-time special education teacher by day and the family glue by night. To this day, I still don't understand how she kept everything going and yet remained tranquil and always available to just talk.

After family dinner and homework were done, she would make a cup of tea and retreat to our living room. In this space, my siblings and I learned that we could come talk to Mom without judgment, shame, or fear. She would listen and ask questions. She was fully present. You left the living room with a plan to resolve whatever issue you faced and an overwhelming sense of love. Mom would shower you with love—a love that came in many forms but at its core was pure love that changed how you felt about yourself and your circumstances.

Later in life, I asked her how she was able to share so much love with all four of her children. She simply said that we all have an endless well of love within us, and it is available to tap and share if you allow it. What an incredible life lesson: You always have more love available to share with yourself, your loved ones, and the world.

Now I have my own beautiful symphony of chaos—two children, a few companies, a passion for endurance athletics, and the list goes on. At the center of this is my boulder, Ashley Mae. We met on the second day of college and married five years later. Since then, we've had careers, started a family, and become entrepreneurs together. We are best friends who work together, raise a family together, and have found a way to live with joy along this journey.

Ashley has a unique spirit that embraces clapping with excitement, setting crazy-huge goals, taking massive action, speaking her mind, smiling all the time, and loving without restraint. She constantly pushes the limits of achievement but does so with infectious joy. She isn't afraid to take immediate action and learn through trial, yet she does it with methodical precision. She is the one-and-only Ashley Mae. She is true to her authentic self and unapologetic about it. What a powerful life lesson—a lesson that most know but so few put into action regularly and find solace in it.

After reconnecting with her authentic self, Ashley has grown as a wife, mom, thought leader, and visionary. But she didn't stop there. She shares her gift with others, and that is where the magic happens. Most people don't realize they are being coached to be true to themselves and embrace it. It is a process that takes time and a lot of positive reinforcement. Watching Ashley do this with family, friends, and colleagues has been a great life lesson. When you find one of your superpowers, share it with the world and allow it to elevate others. Then watch the positive, compounding impact.

Mom and Ashley Mae: Thank you for being you and sharing your authentic, endless love with me and the world. I love you. Shine on.

Mike Volpe

Mike Volpe is CEO of Lola.com, the corporate travel platform that saves companies and their employees time and money on business travel. Previously, he was CMO of cybersecurity company Cybereason, which uncovered a major hack of one of the world's largest wireless companies. He was also part of the founding team at HubSpot, where he served as CMO for eight years while the company grew from $0 to $150 million in annual revenue. He serves on the board of directors of Validity and Privy and has made over forty angel investments. He is known for holding open office hours for anyone in the Boston tech community, with half the time slots reserved for people from underrepresented groups.

. . . .

I am tremendously grateful to the Boston tech community.

Since I moved from San Francisco to Boston eighteen years ago, I've learned and grown so much. I've been lucky enough to be part of growing HubSpot from $0 to $150 million in revenue with an initial public offering and multibillion-dollar valuation, to serve on the board of directors of five companies, to be an angel investor in more than forty companies, and—the most important and gratifying experience—to hire, mentor, and coach hundreds of people and then watch them grow to realize their own potential.

All of that happened because I received my own mentoring and support from people more senior than me in the same community, and I owe a debt to all of them. There were the founder and vice president who took a chance on hiring me when I first came to Boston. There was the vice president who gave me my first chance to manage a team of twelve. There were the investors who gave me a shot at being CMO when I had not done it before. There was the management team that convinced an executive that I was indispensable even though he didn't like me and wanted to replace me.

And then there was the time I was fired—by far the most trying time in my career. There were investors, CEOs, and teammates who stood by me. Your text, email, and voice-mail messages came at a critical time. Although

I was not in a place to thank most of you back then, I appreciate every single message of support. And today there are the investors, employees, and a founder who gave me the chance to be CEO at Lola.com and who continue to support me as we grow.

All these people gave their valuable time instantly and openly, without any expectations. There are too many people to name them individually, but I also know that they don't want the recognition. They take pride in just helping. The thing I love most about the Boston tech community is the complete lack of pretense. West Coast tech companies have a "fake it until you make it" mentality, while Boston entrepreneurs are much more grounded. Ask Bay Area founders how their business is doing, and they'll say, "We're crushing it! All our metrics are off the charts!" Ask Boston founders the same question (for a business with the same metrics), and they'll say, "We're doing well, but we have a lot to work on." Both statements might be true, but there is a humble and realistic element to the Boston response that I love.

To everyone who has helped support me in my journey, thank you. I'm doing my best to pay it forward by being an advisor, angel investor, and coach to other entrepreneurs in Boston.

Stephanie Wiseman

Stephanie Wiseman is a former developer turned business development executive who specializes in digital product development, technology, and brand strategy. She has worked at leading agencies, including BBDO, Work and Co., and DigitasLBi, and she has focused on digital transformation, product strategy and design, plus software-as-a-service solutions. She is currently vice president of business development at YML. Throughout her career, she has been a fierce advocate for technology that enables exceptional customer experiences. She has an extensive background in e-commerce and retail, and her client partners span various industries and include Louis Vuitton, Citibank, Ralph Lauren, Cartier, Columbia Sportswear, and Bloomingdale's/Macy's.

. . . .

I am lucky to say that I have two grandfathers who couldn't be more different in style yet so similar in values. Each has impacted my life tremendously.

My "Grampy" Allen, on my mother's side, sadly passed away when I was sixteen. A humble family man, he worked his way up the ranks as a sales executive for a lighting company. And instead of taking a big promotion that would require relocation, he opened his own business—Rudolph Electric—so that he could help take care of his ailing father-in-law. My grandfather made it clear that you should lead with integrity, you don't have to be a jerk to get ahead, and family should always come first.

My other grandfather—Irving Wiseman—is the man who comes to mind when you think of an executive. At eighty-six years old, he still enters a room with gravitas. He exudes the old adage is true that men want to be him, and women want to be with him.

Irving is direct, whip smart, and personable. Just like Allen, he was a successful salesman when he decided to start his own venture. He created Mercury International, which helped set up the infrastructure and manufacturing for Reebok and other major shoe brands in Southeast Asia. He was a natural and totally crushed it building an international business that allowed for a lifestyle no one could have imagined possible for our family—which was always his driver and primary focus at the end of the day.

Irving and Allen gave me so many life lessons in their own ways:

Money is not everything, but it's okay to focus on it. With 80 percent or more of your time spent at work, why not make the most of it? Cater to your strengths, and earnings will follow. There is no shame in this because wealth can be used to do exciting things with the ones you love, support meaningful causes, and help those in times of need.

A good example of this is how my Papa Irving gifted me my first laptop when I was incredibly sick in the hospital at the age of nine so I could instant-message with my friends. It was a large gesture that he knew would bring joy but also made me feel supported during such a difficult time. Also, it was my first computer, and that's where I learned how to code, which I'm convinced enabled me to progress in my current career.

Don't be boring. Irving and Allen had such different personalities, but they both understand that our time on Earth is short and you should make the most of every moment. For Allen, that included many nights at with his beloved wife, Sylvia, having dinner and talking politics (they always joked they canceled each other's votes). They took vacations regularly where they made lifelong friends, and they were close with every family on their block in Newton, Massachusetts.

Irving is like me (or I'm like him!). We never miss the chance to try a new restaurant, dance at a wedding, or order the nicest glass of wine. He and his wife of more than sixty-five years, Marian, make sure that every night is filled with laughter and vibrancy. They were YOLO-ing before it was a thing.

You can do anything. I am the first grandchild on both sides of my family. And although I can't deny I have been a bit spoiled, there is also an unspoken pressure to carry on the family's legacy. I grew up with two successful examples of entrepreneurs in my life, both of whom took care of their families while also navigating their businesses with ease. They both found ways to support me, encourage me, and tell me that with hard work anything is possible.

One of the most shocking things I experienced when I was a few years into the workforce was the concept of men being treated differently from women. In a way, I was totally sheltered from this. My grandfathers were born in the 1930s, yet they never gave me any indication that I would be anything other than a successful businesswoman.

That blind spot helped me so much in an odd way. I'm not scared to stand up for myself and ask for the raise or extra vacation days. Now one of my favorite things to do is to drag other women along that trajectory with me. It was not a lesson I realized until later in life, but I was given a beautiful gift of progressive, unconditional support.

I fought against myself for a long time. I didn't want to go into sales (working on commission? scary!). But fate has a way of catching up with you. Ten years into my career, I was asked to work as a business development director, and at that moment, I truly became Irving's and Allen's granddaughter—running around to meet others, build businesses, and win accounts. All, of course, while having the most fun possible.

I've never been happier and thank them for giving me their talents and support every step of the way—in more ways than they know.

Jessica Wolf is vice president of SomethingNew. She is also a soul searcher, a mom, a wife to a volunteer firefighter, a friend, and a lifelong learner striving to find balance in this hectic world. Having children and a spouse with a "gotta run, the pager went off" schedule, she has had to learn to adjust to variability and the unknown versus the calculated and planned. She prides herself on building strong relationships and remains true to her character with the unwavering belief that being yourself is always the best way to go.

. . . .

Shortly after I obtained a bachelor's of business administration degree in human resources management, I was on the hunt for an entry-level position in the field. As fate would have it, I hired a woman to help me create a professional résumé that would be more HR-focused, and as we got to know each other a bit, she mentioned that she was working in an HR role at a company that had recently hired a new HR director who was looking to build a strong team. She thought I would be a great fit.

She put my name in for an HR assistant position, and I interviewed for the job shortly after. By nature, I'm highly organized. I clean my pantry and organize my kid's back-to-school gear for fun, people! So I showed up for my first interview at a local coffee shop with my neatly organized portfolio and additional copies of my résumé, notes, pen, paper, questions, etc., all separated by tabs. For the interview, I met the woman who was helping me with my résumé, an HR manager, and the HR director, Mark Elder.

From the time I met Mark in that first interview, I knew he wouldn't be like any other director I had worked for—not only because he loved my tabbed portfolio, but because of how he made me feel while we were talking. He was engaged, genuine, passionate about building a strong team, transparent, and interested in what I had to say.

I got the job, and throughout my time with the organization, Mark's door was always open—to anyone. He listened attentively and made you feel supported. He built a strong HR team and mentored us through the good and the bad. He reminded the team regularly that we weren't paper pushers. Instead, we were strategic business partners who worked closely with all departments across the organization to build strong teams, build trusting and professional relationships, and work together instead of against one another.

During one of our conversations, he asked me what I wanted my legacy to be. I was taken aback. I had never been asked such a thing before and had not given any consideration to it. But I can tell you that question has stuck with me over the years and is something I think about and focus on regularly.

Earlier, I said, "I knew he wouldn't be like any other director I had worked for," but in truth Mark wasn't someone I worked for, he was someone I worked with. It was a true team, and I felt supported and empowered.

If you ask him, he'll tell you his legacy is our legacy, our growth, our success, and our positive and impactful leadership styles. When I think about his leadership style and what contributed to the successes of our team, which rippled across the organization, I can easily see the same traits that I saw during my initial interview. He was always engaged, genuine, passionate, transparent, and interested in what others had to say. And he had fun.

I transitioned out of the organization but remained focused on his question. As I live my life, I have struggled to balance all the responsibilities it brings—self, marriage, motherhood, friendships, career, giving back, and everything else that makes up our days. With that struggle, I initially felt pressure to build legacies both professionally and personally, but as I continue to grow in this life and learn its lessons, I have found that one's legacy doesn't have to differ in our personal and professional lives; it can be one and the same.

I know how I felt when I was empowered and supported in my professional role while working with Mark. I know how I feel when I am encouraged by my husband, family, and friends. And I know how unstoppable I feel when I trust myself to just go. I see how my children—and adults for that matter—shine when they are heard and praised. Being that same empowering, supportive person, that light, that spunk, for others is what I am so grateful to experience. Being present makes a difference. I want this to be my legacy.

How about you? What will your legacy be?

Who are you grateful for?

Who in your life deserves a standing O?
Don't let time slip by—let them know today!

About Look for the Good Project _LookForTheGoodProject.org_

Look for the Good Project is a Connecticut-based nonprofit organization that empowers children to run school-wide gratitude and kindness campaigns.

Our mission is to make America kind, one school at a time. We build our programming around the core belief that gratitude changes mindsets, reduces violence, and improves everything. In just three years, our elementary school program has reached 121,545 students in 30 states, who have written almost 2 million messages of gratitude to uplift their school communities.

Of the 2,600 students who opted to take our anonymous survey, 76% of students reported there was more kindness in the school, 71% thought there was less bullying during the program, and 92% reported that they would recommend the program to other schools. Feedback from school staff has been 100% positive, and many schools opt to run the program year after year!

To sponsor a Look for the Good Program at a school near you, please contact our office at the Connecticut Association of Schools:

Look for the Good Project
30 Realty Drive
Cheshire, CT 06410
info@lookforthegood.org

Made in the USA
Monee, IL
29 October 2021

06971fbd-d923-4233-8b31-93b9afb99a06R01